GAME GURU

STRATEGY GAMES

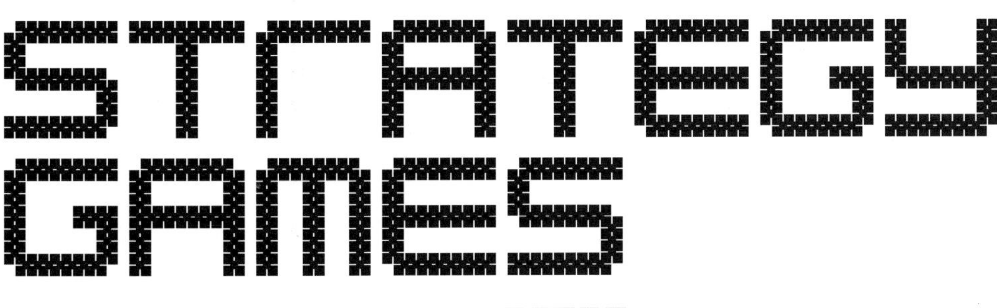

DAVE MORRIS AND LEO HARTAS

ILEX

First published in the United Kingdom
in 2004 by
ILEX
The Old Candlemakers,
West Street,
Lewes,
East Sussex,
BN7 2NZ
www.ilex-press.com

This book was conceived by
ILEX, Cambridge, England

Publisher: Alastair Campbell
Executive Publisher: Sophie Collins
Creative Director: Peter Bridgewater
Editor: Stuart Andrews
Design Manager: Tony Seddon
Designer: Jonathan Raimes
Artwork Assistant: Joanna Clinch
Development Art Director: Graham Davis
Technical Art Editor: Nicholas Rowland

British Library Cataloguing-in-Publication Data
A catalogue record for this book is available from the British Library

ISBN 1-904705-31-6

Printed and bound in China

For more on strategy games visit:
www.ggstuk.web-linked.com

PREFACE

As any art form evolves, people start to analyse what is going on there under the bonnet. We are interested in finding out what makes the best examples work, so that we can try to make more compelling films or novels or games in the future.

The trap is when analysis becomes dry and academic. This is what we have striven to avoid with the Game Guru series. Our aim is not to create a series of textbooks where the obsessive picking apart of detail can obscure the bigger picture. Instead, we are presenting the reader with what we hope will be a thought-provoking overview of each genre.

Criticism in art is not just about judgment, or saying what is good or bad. Criticism should also have the goal of promoting understanding. The critical viewer or reader or player is one who will demand higher standards, which benefits us all. In the Game Guru series we hope to impart insights that will help designers and players alike to take a clearer view of what works in games, and why.

If you are a designer, we want to help you make better games. If you are a player, we want to help you enjoy games more. And no matter who you are, we want Game Gurus to stimulate your enthusiasm for the medium of gaming. Because what games will become over the next century is up to you.

DAVE MORRIS AND **LEO HARTAS**

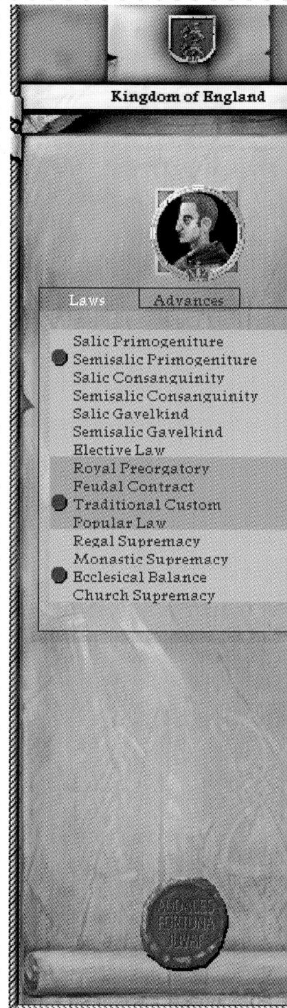

Crusader Kings
Paradox.

ONLY A SHORT TIME AGO, COMPUTER AND VIDEOGAMES WERE REGARDED AS A TRIVIAL PASTIME. NOW, ONLY THE MOST DOGGED REACTIONARY WOULD REFUSE TO RECOGNISE THAT THEY HAVE BECOME AN ART FORM IN THEIR OWN RIGHT. ONE WHO SAYS, 'OH, I DON'T PLAY GAMES' IS LIKE A THEATRE SNOB OF THE EARLY 20TH CENTURY REFUSING TO ENTER A CINEMA – AND THEREBY MISSING OUT ON THE EXCITEMENT OF AN ENTERTAINMENT REVOLUTION.

CONTENTS

INTRODUCTION 6

SECTION 1 WAR 8

1 UNITS AND ATTRIBUTES 12
2 COMBINED ARMS 22
3 THE LIE OF THE LAND 30
4 THE MAIN CHANCE 42
5 DEFENCE 48

SECTION 2 PEACE 50

6 RESOURCES 52
7 HOME 64
8 THE FOG OF WAR 68
9 TECHNOLOGY 72
10 SUPPLY 80

SECTION 3 DESIGN 86

11 INTERFACE 88
12 BALANCE 96
13 CAMPAIGNS AND LEVELS 98
14 SCALE 106
15 STYLE 110
16 GAMEPLAY 114
17 SETTINGS 120
18 THE FUTURE 130
GLOSSARY AND INDEX 140
ACKNOWLEDGEMENTS 144

STRATEGY IS THE ART OF SOLVING PROBLEMS. MORE PEDANTICALLY, STRATEGIC THINKING INVOLVES ANALYSING A COMPLEX PROBLEM DOMAIN AND EVOLVING A METHODOLOGY, OR STRATEGY, FOR SOLVING IT. 'A METHOD IS NEEDED IN ORDER TO REASON ACCURATELY', WROTE DESCARTES.

MORE PERTINENTLY TO THE SUBJECT UNDER DISCUSSION, CARL VON CLAUSEWITZ SAID: 'STRATEGY IS THE PLAN OF THE WAR'. IF YOU SUBSTITUTE THE WORD 'CONFLICT' FOR WAR – WHERE 'CONFLICT' ALLOWS A BROAD ENOUGH INTERPRETATION TO INCLUDE CHALLENGES OF EXPLORATION AND SURVIVAL POSED BY THE ENVIRONMENT AND BLIND FATE – THEN CLAUSEWITZ'S DEFINITION IS ON THE MONEY.

STRATEGY GAMES DIFFER FROM SIMPLE PUZZLE GAMES. TYPICALLY, PUZZLES ARE NON-COMPLEX. PUZZLES MIGHT BE COMPLICATED TO SOLVE, BUT THAT'S SOMETHING ELSE. COMPLEXITY MEANS THAT THE CONDITIONS OF THE PROBLEM DOMAIN ARE NOT SIMPLE RESTATEMENTS OF THE UNDERLYING RULES. IN OTHER WORDS, IN STRATEGY GAMES, THE PROBLEM REQUIRING SOLUTION OUGHT TO BE EMERGENT FROM ANOTHER SET OF CAUSES.

WHY IS THIS A REQUIREMENT? THE ANSWER IS THAT WE HUMANS ENJOY ACQUIRING AN INTUITIVE GRASP OF COMPLEX PROBLEMS. THE CHESS PLAYER EXPERIENCES THIS WHEN HE OR SHE GLANCES AT A BOARD AND KNOWS AT ONCE WHO IS WINNING. STRATEGY IS THE PLEASURE OF SEEING THE BIG PICTURE.

THE PROBLEM DOMAIN IS AN ABSTRACTION THAT DISTILS A SCENARIO DOWN TO ITS INTERESTING ELEMENTS. IT COULD BE A MATHEMATICAL MODEL OF THE ECONOMY, IN WHICH CASE THE STRATEGIES INVOLVED ARE THE GOVERNMENT'S PROJECTIONS FOR TAXATION AND PUBLIC SPENDING. IN STRATEGY GAMES ALL KINDS OF SUB-GENRES ARE POSSIBLE.

'NO ONE ELEMENT FORMS THE HEART OF STRATEGY GAMES. THE MAIN OBJECTIVE IS TO ENCOURAGE THE PLAYER TO MAKE DECISIONS AND FORM A STRATEGY. AN IMPORTANT PRACTICAL POINT TO NOTE WHEN MAKING A GAME IS ENSURING THAT, IF YOU GO TO THE EFFORT OF IMPLEMENTING A SPECIFIC ELEMENT (BUILDING STRUCTURES, STRATEGIC BENEFITS FOR EXPLORATION, TACTICAL COMBAT), THEN THE PLAYER MUST CLEARLY UNDERSTAND THE CHOICES YOU ARE PRESENTING AND SHOULD GAIN ENJOYMENT FROM MAKING THE CHOICE. YOU ALSO HAVE TO ENSURE THAT, IF YOU HAVE MORE THAN ONE ELEMENT, THEY WORK TOGETHER. YOU COULD SAY THAT THE HEART OF THE STRATEGY GAME IS MADE UP OF COMPONENTS, AND TO FUNCTION PROPERLY THOSE COMPONENTS NEED TO WORK IN HARMONY.'
PAUL TWYNHOLM, LEAD DESIGNER AT CLIMAX

Left: ***Spellforce: The Order of Dawn***. *Phenomic.*

Above: ***Gettysberg***. *Firaxis.* ***Command & Conquer: Generals***. *EA Pacific.* ***Haegemonia***. *DigitalReality.*

Desert Rats vs. Afrika Corps
from Digital Reality

SECTION 1

WAR

COMPUTER STRATEGY GAMES CAN TRACE THEIR LINE OF DESCENT FROM THE MONUMENTAL HEX–GRID BOARDGAMES USED TO SIMULATE GRAND SWATHES OF HISTORY SUCH AS THE RISE AND THE FALL OF THE ROMAN EMPIRE OR, ON AN ONLY MARGINALLY LESS GRANDIOSE SCALE, THE CAMPAIGNS OF NAPOLEON.

IT IS THEREFORE NOT SURPRISING THAT THE EMPHASIS IN THE GENRE HAS BEEN ON WAR. WHEN YOU ARE FACING ANOTHER PLAYER ACROSS A PAPER MAP AND YOUR DICE AND COUNTERS ARE TO HAND, THERE CAN BE ONLY ONE WINNER. APPEASEMENT IS FOR WIMPS.

WHEN THE GENRE MOVED OVER INTO THE NEW MEDIUM OF COMPUTER GAMES, THAT ALL CHANGED – POTENTIALLY AT LEAST. WITHOUT THE NEED FOR HUMAN OPPONENTS, THE NATURE OF THE ENTERTAINMENT COULD CHANGE. STRATEGY-FLAVORED VARIANTS OF SOLITAIRE ALLOW THE PLAYER TO EXPLORE AND COLONIZE THE NEW WORLD, TO MANAGE A CITY OR AN AMUSEMENT PARK, TO BECOME AN ANT OR A GOD – OR ANYTHING IN BETWEEN.

CONFLICT REMAINED AT THE CORE OF STRATEGY, BUT NOW CONFLICT WAS OPEN TO WIDER INTERPRETATION. INSTEAD OF AN ADVERSARY INTENT ON CONQUEST, THE CONFLICT MIGHT COME FROM MANAGING TENSIONS WITHIN THE GAME – MAKING YOUR POPULACE BOTH HAPPY AND HARD-WORKING, FOR EXAMPLE, OR FINDING A HAPPY MEDIUM BETWEEN ECONOMIC GROWTH AND STABILITY. SO STRATEGY TOOK A FEW STEPS INTO THE MANAGEMENT GENRE, BUT HUMAN NATURE DOESN'T CHANGE. THE REAL ALLURE WILL ALWAYS BE WAR. CLAUSEWITZ FAMOUSLY DECLARED WAR TO BE THE CONTINUATION OF POLITICS WITH THE ADMIXTURE OF OTHER MEANS. IN THE CASE OF MOST STRATEGY GAMES WE CAN REVERSE THAT. POLITICS EXPLORATION, DIPLOMACY AND TRADE ARE ALL JUST PRELUDES TO WAR.

'KILL THEM ALL. GOD WILL KNOW HIS OWN.'
ARNAUD AMAURY

'WHEN THE ENEMY ADVANCES, WITHDRAW. WHEN HE STOPS, HARASS. WHEN HE TIRES, STRIKE. WHEN HE RETREATS, PURSUE.' MAO TSE TUNG

Even the most beatific pacifist can see the appeal. You are a commander of armies and you are fighting to become ruler of the entire world – even if that world is just a single map the size of a football field. In true strategy games you plan the spread of your empire, choosing your battles and advancing ruthlessly against your rivals. Daring, timing and tactics are the keys to victory. There can be only one winner and you are determined to be that one. The play intention at the heart of strategy is to make yourself master of all you survey.

Strategy is not the same as tactics. Tactics deal with the way you deploy the troops you have in a given battle. Strategy views the bigger picture, determining not only the mix of troops you bring to that battle, and the place you choose to fight, but your overall doctrine of war and the way you set about achieving your goals.

'THE MOST CERTAIN WAY OF ENSURING VICTORY IS TO MARCH BRISKLY AND IN GOOD ORDER AGAINST THE ENEMY, ALWAYS ENDEAVOURING TO GAIN GROUND.' *FREDERICK THE GREAT*

The goals themselves are usually set by the victory conditions of the game. Total destruction of the foe is not only unrealistic; it also tends to create a drawn-out endgame by forcing the winning player to scour the map looking for every last enemy soldier who must be wiped out to trigger victory.

Preferable is some form of partial victory or a specific condition that will cause computer opponents to surrender. You can also legitimately apply this to human-controlled troops. Why should they not throw down their arms when the cause becomes hopeless, after all? It's a good feature to thwart the occasional never-say-die human player who derives warped solace from forcing his opponent to play on long after the outcome of the game is obvious.

'IF AN INJURY HAS TO BE DONE TO A MAN, IT SHOULD BE SO SEVERE THAT HIS VENGEANCE NEED NOT BE FEARED.' NICCOLO MACHIAVELLI

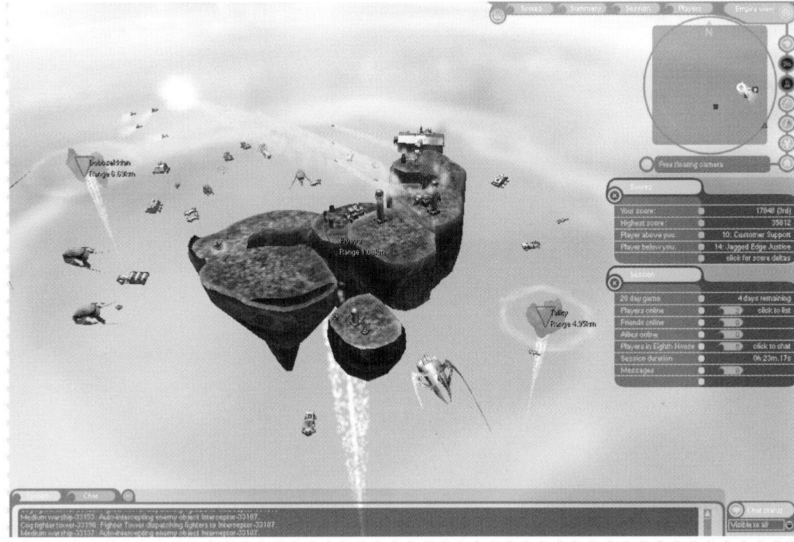

Above: ***Time of Defiance*** *from Nicely Crafted Entertainment.*

Below: ***Against Rome*** *by Independent Arts.*

Specific goals are common in campaign levels, especially in games with an explicitly historical basis. Here the player must satisfy an objective in order to win. For example, holding a bridge for 20 minutes, gathering 500 units of gold, capturing all ten sacred relics, or building a 'wonder of the world'.

Some games allow players to define their own objectives. This can create interesting gameplay but needs to be handled adroitly. The different objectives must be of equivalent difficulty. Also, there need to be clues that will allow opponents to deduce the player's customised victory condition. Then the tension between achieving the objective and disguising it becomes a matter of strategic thought. If the objective can abruptly be accomplished without the other players having any chance to anticipate or counter it, the feature of being able to choose the objective adds nothing but an element of luck. And it isn't luck that's bad in a strategy game, only luck in the absence of anything else.

Above: ***War Times*** *by IS Games.*

Right: *CDV Software's* ***Codename: Panzers.***

Homeworld 2 by Relic

UNITS AND ATTRIBUTES

GAME DESIGN INVOLVES CHOOSING A LEVEL OF ABSTRACTION THAT ALLOWS USERS TO PLAY AROUND WITH THE INTERESTING ELEMENTS OF A SCENARIO WHILE NOT HAVING TO BOTHER ABOUT THE CLUTTER. WHAT THE DESIGNER IDENTIFIES AS IMPORTANT – THE QUINTESSENTIAL ELEMENTS THAT HE OR SHE USES TO DEFINE UNITS (CHARACTERS) AND ATTRIBUTES IN THE GAME ABSTRACTION – IMPLY A DIRECTION AND EMPHASIS FOR THE GAMEPLAY.

Say you're setting out to create a game called *In Tents*, the strategy game of camping trips. Characters have to complete various tasks to stay happy and healthy. Just considering the physical attributes of the campers, you're going to need to define things like speed (how fast the character moves), appetite (how much food the character needs), stamina (how long a character can stay active before needing a nap), strength (governs tasks like chopping wood, the loads the character can carry, etc.) and aim (accuracy of shooting gun or bow).

But how many attributes do you need? Too many and your game becomes a distinctly solitary vice. On the other hand, too few and there's going to be no depth of gameplay. Also, some of the attributes may be derived from or interdependent on others. For instance, stamina is the rate at which the character uses up energy. We might expect high strength or speed to burn up energy faster, and so give lower stamina. That's potentially interesting for gameplay purposes – it means that it's wasteful to use the strongest character for light tasks that a couple of weaker characters could handle. But it also means we've jumped a level of abstraction, and while this is OK as far as the player is concerned, it still needs to be thought through in the ur-design – the underlying design layer – or it could lead to more serious problems later.

'Each unit should always come with a price tag: resources, spawning time, upgrades, sacrificed units. Also, the unit should have a weakness. A powerful ground unit may not be able to attack airborne units, for example. For a unit to be valid there must be way to counter it.'

DANNY BELANGER

Director of Internal Development at Strategy First

Below: ***Magic & Mayhem: The Art of Magic*** *from Climax. Units are conjured up by wizards to be sent into battle.*

Bottom: ***Codename: Panzers*** *from CDV Software.*

SOME PHYSICISTS EXPLAIN THE COMPLEXITY OF THE UNIVERSE AS A RESULT OF OUR SEEING ONLY PART OF A BIGGER PICTURE. THEY USE THE SO-CALLED 'SUPERSTRING' MODEL, WHICH REQUIRES THE DEEPER UNIVERSE TO OPERATE IN 12 OR MORE DIMENSIONS, OF WHICH WE ONLY EXPERIENCE THE FOUR DIMENSIONS OF SPACE-TIME.

GORDIAN KNOTS

It may well be that the design of the universe requires 12 dimensions. Game design needs to be a lot more streamlined, however, to avoid getting tied in knots. Here's why.

Imagine a game with just three attributes: defence, attack and speed. It's very abstract but you can still see the bare bones of how the game would work. A unit with just defence is a bunker. A unit with just attack is artillery. A unit with just speed is a scout.

Let's consider just the combinations of units with one fixed build cost. Say that each unit can have attributes totalling to 3. So (3,0,0) is the bunker, (0,3,0) is the artillery, and so on. The most versatile unit – the jack-of-all trades – is (1,1,1). Taking only integral values for the attributes, there are ten combinations – that is, ten different units with a build cost of 3.

OK, so here's the thing. Ten units means ten first-order strategies – that is, strategies at the level where you are simply picking a specific unit for a specific job.

However, first-order strategies are usually trivial. You can work them out from simple algorithms. In most games it's the higher-order strategies that yield the interesting choices that define good gameplay. Higher-order strategies involve combined arms, where you might, for example, be sending a wave of scouts ahead of light fighters who will aim to pin down enemy patrols long enough for your slower, heavy fighters to arrive on the scene.

How many higher-order strategies can you get with ten different units? The fact is, there's no finite solution. In practice a human player is mostly going to be thinking in terms of armies comprising three or four different unit types at most, so a rule of thumb answer would be around two dozen strategies – but that's a broad guesstimate that still doesn't allow for the numbers of units of each type.

The bottom line is that if just three attributes can potentially yield a few dozen strategies, you can see that you don't need many for rich gameplay. Stephen Wolfram, the creator of Mathematica, has proposed that the complex

Right: ***Savage: The Battle for Newerth*** *by S2 Games. Online massively multiplayer games are becoming more common. The variables of unit strengths and weaknesses become infinitely complex when all the players are human.*

Below: ***Massive Assault*** *from Wargaming.net*

ATTACK

SPEED

DEFENCE

The attribute space for a simple wargame. Note that there are two ways that a unit should be balanced. First the designer needs to consider the resource cost of building the armour that gives DEFENCE, propulsion that yields SPEED and weaponry from which ATTACK is derived. (Looking at the equivalent case in nature, there is a cost for building bones and thick hide and muscles and sharp claws, and the animal needs to be able to acquire sufficient calories to sustain that growth.) Upgrades typically allow a more efficient propulsion system, etc., to be built at lower resource cost. The other type of balance is a consequence of the physics. More armour means more mass, which means spending more on propulsion just to keep the same SPEED. Formerly, the designer would pre-calculate all this in the ur-design (which usually meant the backs of many envelopes) before writing the resulting attribute values into the design. Today, it is possible to model the underlying physics so that the attributes are derived at runtime.

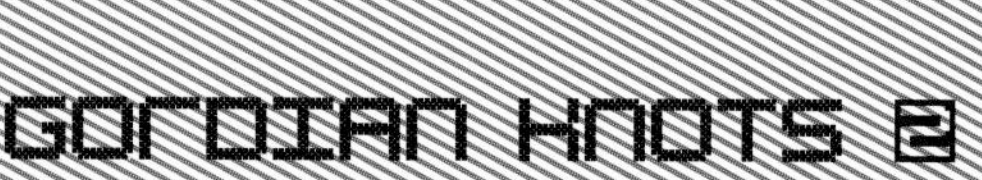

Below: *Blizzard, specialists i the real-time strategy genre are renowned for precise balance of units.* ***Warcraft 3*** *is the latest in a distinguishe line of titles.*

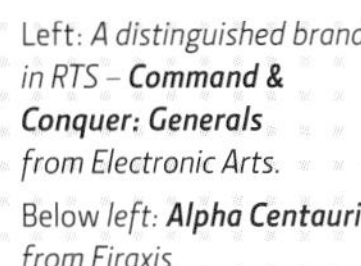

Left: *A distinguished brand in RTS* – ***Command & Conquer: Generals*** *from Electronic Arts.*

Below left: ***Alpha Centauri*** *from Firaxis*

phenomenon we call the universe is not a view from underneath of a twelve-dimensional meta-reality. It may instead be the emergent result of just a very few simpler rules or dimensions. Whether or not Wolfram's model is how the universe works, it's a good template for game design.

Summing up: the attributes used in a strategy game define the characters (or units) for the player and imply a direction and emphasis for the game. Attributes measure the unit's capacity in each of the dimensions of the game abstraction. The interaction between the attributes is what creates the potential for strategy – and a small number of attributes can quickly lead to a very large number of strategies.

A large number of strategies requires balancing at the design stage because it is important to avoid dominant or dominated strategies. Dominant strategies are those that are always worth choosing no matter what the opponent does. Dominated strategies are those that are never worth choosing under any circumstances. Both sound like they'd be easy to avoid but in fact either type can slip in through the net while your attention is on another part of the design. Both are design killers because the work implemented is wasted. For example, if the use of incendiary pigs is a dominated strategy, then all the modelling and animation the artists did for incendiary pigs and the cool particle effects for them bursting into flames will never get seen.

Complex design creates exponential problems of balance. The tricky part is that rich gameplay often derives from complexity. It's when you see the emergent possibilities for new strategies that you get that special sense of cunning delight unique to hunters and gamers. However, by no means all complex gameplay is rich or rewarding. Sometimes it really is just a mess of knots that need cutting.

Left: *Westwood's* ***Earth & Beyond.***

AT THE TOP OF THE TECH TREE LURKS SOMETHING THAT SHOULD SCARE THE RTS DESIGNER MORE THAN ANY NIGHTMARE CREATION OF EDWARD GOREY OR MAURICE SENDAK. THIS IS THE SUPER UNIT, THE KILLER TROOP TYPE, THE NONPAREIL CHARACTER WHO STOMPS AND CRUSHES ALL IN HIS PATH.

SUPER UNITS

Above & Far right: *Games get truly epic.* ***Age of Mythology: The Titans*** *by Ensemble.*

'SUPER UNITS ARE A CARRY-OVER FROM THE SINGLE-PLAYER RTS AND DON'T HAVE A PLACE IN A BALANCED PLAYER VS. PLAYER SITUATION. BY ALL MEANS LET PLAYERS UNLOCK NEW AND ADVANCED UNITS, BUT THEY SHOULDN'T BE UNDEFEATABLE.'
MARK ASHTON SENIOR PRODUCER AT NICELY CRAFTED ENTERTAINMENT

Below left: ***Command & Conquer: Generals*** *from EA Pacific. Going nuclear is the present-day version of the super-unit. As in real life, once both sides start using nukes there are no winners.*

Below: *Chap with the metal head, five rounds rapid.* ***Silent Storm*** *by Nival.*

The super unit dominates all others. He strides the land like a colossus, steamrolling enemies and the need for combined arms or any other strategic doctrine into the ground. He is nimbler than a skirmisher, outranges longbowmen, outguns artillery, scythes down infantry faster than Sauron with a Sabatier knife.

The original *Warcraft* featured two super units: demons and elementals. In the early stages of a game you had three units with a very elegant relationship among them. Knights were shot to pieces by archers, archers were blown to smithereens by catapults and knights chopped up catapults in short order. (There were also footmen, in fact, but they were effectively a cheaper, weaker, slower version of knights.)

The tactical possibilities emerging from just that simple three-way Condorcet Cycle (*see p25*) were very rich, making the original *Warcraft* still one of the best RTS games of all time. Tactics went out of the window, however, once a player got far enough along to start conjuring demons or elementals. These units could kill anything else with impunity. Victory then became a question of spawning as many mages as you could in order to conjure an army of demons.

'SUPER UNITS CAN BE ENTERTAINING AS ONE-OFF EASTER EGGS. THEY SHOULD NOT BE PART OF THE STANDARD GAME.'
FREDRIK LINDGREN OF PARADOX

'SOME PLAYERS LIKE ACQUIRING THE SUPER UNITS, BUT THEY UNBALANCE THE GAME AND MAKE THE BATTLE ASPECTS LESS INTERESTING. IT IS GOOD TO HAVE SPECIAL UNITS WHICH PROVIDE MORE POSSIBILITIES AND STRATEGIES, BUT NOT SUPER UNITS WITH NO WEAKNESS.'
IGNACIO PÉREZ STUDIO DIRECTOR AT PYRO STUDIOS

SUPER UNITS 2

To get a really rewarding game of *Warcraft*, you had to disallow demons and elementals. Once in play, they obviated the need for tactics – and it was the tactics that made *Warcraft* great. So, were those super units in *Warcraft* too tough? Actually, you could argue that they weren't tough enough.

Think of it this way. The super unit can be a useful design device to create positive feedback in the endgame. In that sense it would be just like building a wonder in *Age of Empires*. The entire game then becomes an econo-military race to be able to build the winning totem – which could be a wonder, or a super unit, or the spaceship that colonises Alpha Centauri.

Used that way, the super unit is good because it's a fun, dramatic way to force the game to a clear conclusion. The actual process of stomping the other player back to the Stone Age is then just a foregone conclusion, a big bang of a reward for winning the race.

The problem is when the super unit is dominant over all other units, but not powerful enough to deliver the killer punch. Then both sides end up with super units. Now, because other units are all inferior, the players staff their entire army with the super unit. The game continues and drags on with no hope of the accelerating pace needed for a good endgame. And even worse, in place of interesting tactics and the possibility of a strategic masterstroke to finish things off, it gets bogged down in a tedious slugfest between the super units.

If you're designing a strategy game and you're thinking about having a super unit, be bold. A tough but inconclusive super unit will break your game. If you want it to have a valid role, it has to be truly godlike.

Above: *Heroes in a whole shell from Relic's* ***Impossible Creatures***.

Top: *You have 15 seconds to comply in **MechAssault** from Day 1 Studios.*

Above: *The barnstormingly different **Project Nomads** from Radon Labs.*

COMBINED ARMS

IN REAL LIFE, WEAPON SYSTEMS REQUIRE THE USE OF A MIXTURE OF UNITS OF DIFFERENT TYPES TO ACHIEVE A GOAL. THIS IS THE ASPECT OF WAR THAT IS CLOSEST TO GAME THEORY, AND PROVIDES USEFUL LESSONS FOR THE STRATEGY DESIGNER.

Above: ***Massive Assault.*** *Wargaming.net*

Above: Icon from ***Gettysberg*** *from Firaxis*

Cyclical relationships ensure there is no 'best' troop type, ensuring the game will allow for and encourage tactics. A simple combined arms weapon system based on the familiar Paper-Scissors-Stone game mechanic can lead to unexpected richness and variety.

'Combined arms systems challenge the player to balance his own forces while constantly attempting to exploit any imbalance observed in the opponent's force. When you throw terrain modifiers into this, these systems allow incredible tactical depth.'
CHARLIE BEWSHER *Lead Designer at Black Cactus Games*

In order for a game to encourage interesting tactics, there can't be a single best unit. If tanks always beat infantry and there's nothing an infantryman can do that a tank can't, then the use of tanks is said to be a dominant strategy. Players won't use the dominated choice, so it was a waste of time putting it in the game.

'Attributes need to be balanced so that no single unit type can dominate completely, and the easiest way of balancing is the classic trade-off: stronger means slower and so on.'
FREDRIK LINDGREN *of Paradox Entertainment*

On the other hand, suppose the infantry are quicker and can cross terrain such as sand or marshland where a tank would get bogged down. And the tank fires more slowly but its shells do more damage, making it useful against armoured targets and buildings that the infantryman cannot affect. Now we have the elements of a combined arms system. To win, a player must assemble a force comprising several different troop types, and must use each to best advantage. This is the very essence of tactics.

The classic combined arms relationship can be expressed with three troop types: archers, footmen and cavalry. Archers beat footmen because (wearing no armour) they can retreat swiftly and shoot at the footmen from a distance. Footmen beat cavalry because they wear heavier armour and can fight in closer formation. But cavalry beat archers because the horses are swifter than even unarmoured men, and therefore they can run them down.

Below: ***Laser Squad: Nemesis*** *by Codo International*

Left: *Concept sketches from* ***Silent Storm*** *by Nival Interactive.*

The classic combined arms relationship has been manifest in many forms throughout history. When technology evolves one troop type in advance of others, dominated strategies can temporarily occur until a further invention restores parity. Advances in artillery firepower in the early part of the 20th century made heavily dug-in defences the only option, leading to the impasse of WWI. It was only with the arrival of tanks and aircraft that the deadlock could be broken.

COMBINED ARMS 2

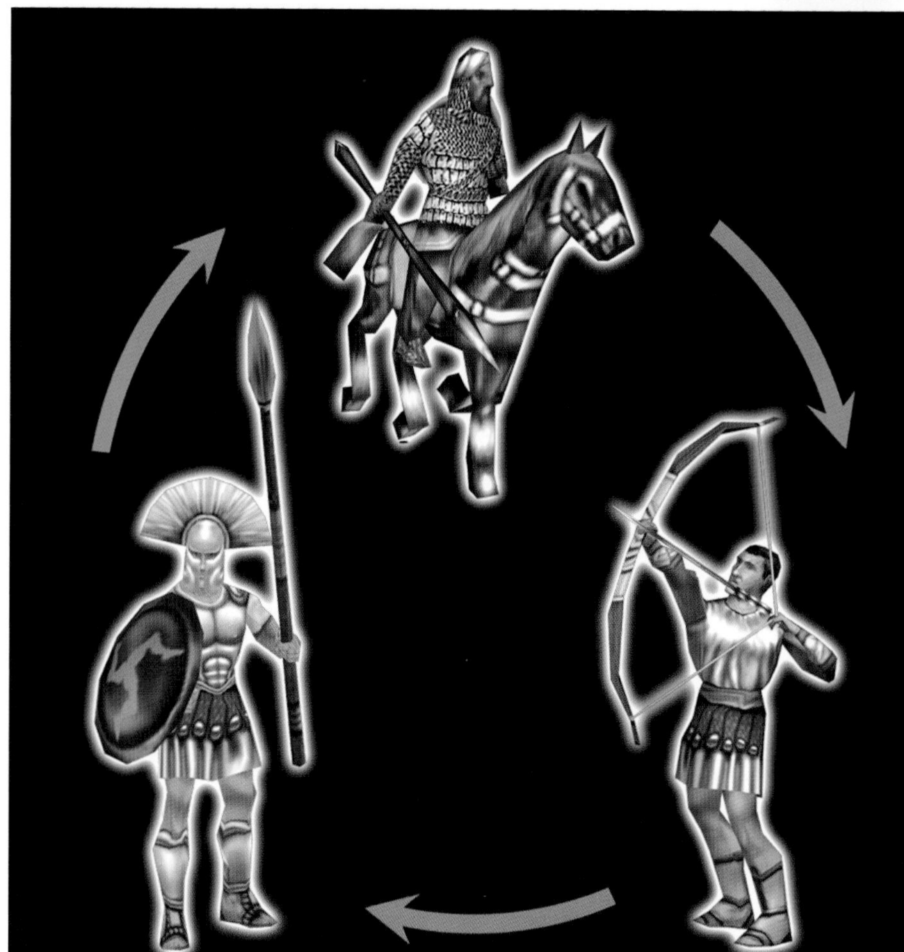

That same Paper-Scissors-Stone dynamic can be applied to any historical period or theatre of war. Tanks beat anti-aircraft guns beat aircraft beat tanks. Battleships beat destroyers beat submarines beat battleships. And so on. In game theoretic analysis this kind of intransitive relationship is known as a Condorcet Cycle.

However, a Condorcet Cycle is only the minimum you need for interesting tactical gameplay. It would be pretty dull if all a player had to do was to be sure to spawn equal numbers of each type.

Combined arms relationships in practice aren't solely fixed by the inherent attributes of units; they arise out of the physics of the game. And that provides the key to interesting gameplay, because then a player can use the physical characteristics of the battlefield to modify the capabilities of his troops. Terrain and deployment are the most obvious modifying factors. Infantry on high ground have less to fear from archers shooting up at them – the force of the arrows is spent fighting gravity. The Spartans used a narrow pass at Thermopylae that denied the Persians the benefit of their vastly superior numbers. And slingers deployed behind palings or quagmire can do very well against cavalry.

Weather effects are also significant. Thick fog robs ranged-weapon troops like archers of their effectiveness – they can't shoot what they can't see. Early gunpowder weapons are also badly affected by damp and cold.

Condorcet (intransitive) Cycles can be more complex than basic Paper Scissors Stone. This shows a five-way system among crossbowmen, horse archers, infantry, heavy cavalry and medieval artillery (in this case a naphtha-thrower). Note that none of these troop types is dominant.

Napoleon's army at Moscow found their guns falling apart in the Russian winter. Night attacks favour cavalry, since horses can see in the dark even if their riders cannot.

A richly detailed physics system therefore produces emergent results of which the classic combined arms diagram seen here is merely the simplest case. A clever player will watch for modifying factors and so choose the time and place of battle that suits his forces best.

ONE WAY OF LOOKING AT THE UNITS IN A STRATEGY GAME IS TO THINK OF THEM AS SPECIES IN AN ECOSYSTEM. IMAGINE THE ECOSYSTEM AS AN N-DIMENSIONAL SPACE WHERE THE AXES ARE ATTRIBUTES SUCH AS SPEED, STAMINA, ARMOUR, WEAPONRY, HIT POINTS AND SO ON.

STRANGE ATTRACTORS

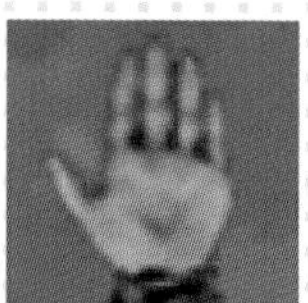

*Blizzard's masterful **Warcraft 3**.*

Top: *Heads up!* ***Silent Storm*** *by Nival.*

Above: *Digital Reality's* ***Platoon*** *evokes many enjoyable afternoons spent painting soldiers.*

Most probably you're now thinking of a three-dimensional space, but that will do!

In evolution, each species must find a niche that will correspond to points in the N-dimensional space. A cheetah is one such. It's fast and light, it runs its prey down and has just enough weaponry to make the kill. Hyenas inhabit another niche – slower, but with the strength of numbers to drive the cheetah off its kill.

The viable strategies are attractor points. In other words, a strategy can be described in terms of a particular combination of attributes. The attractor points are the "Platonic form" of various species. In reality, a species may converge on its nearest attractor point over many generations but it's unlikely ever to reach it. The reason is that the attractor points are in constant motion.

To illustrate, let's look at the hyenas and the cheetah. Before the hyenas arrived, the cheetah could count on getting a large share of each wildebeest he brought down. Vultures would come and scavenge but they are light animals and don't take much. Eventually a solitary lion might wander up but by then the cheetah would have already had rich pickings off the kill.

Now introduce hyenas to the system. They travel in packs, so one locates the kill and calls to others. The pack arrives in force and drives the cheetah off. Instead of getting half the meat from his kill, the cheetah now has to make do with, say, the one quarter he has time to gulp down before the hyenas turn up. A new strategy is needed in response. Remember that by 'strategy" we now don't just mean what the cheetah does (although that's part of it); we also mean what he is. Over generations, cheetahs might become lighter and then require less food – or on the other hand, they might become bigger and tougher, able to fight off hyenas. The hyenas will also adapt over time. Hence the attractor points are in constant motion and you can imagine species trailing along behind them in a millennial orbit.

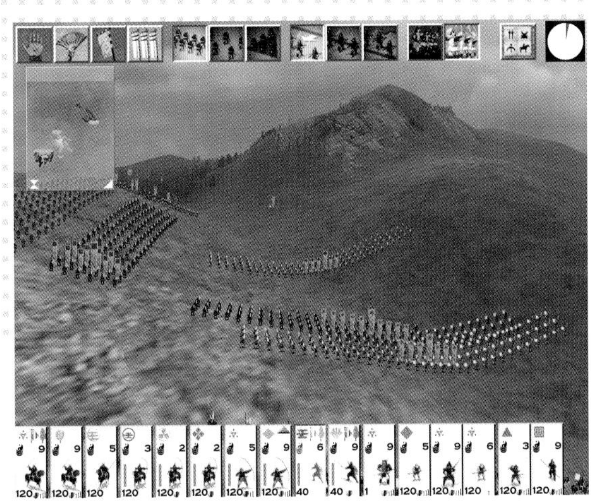

Right: *Creative Assembly's* ***Shogun Total War*** *– an early RTS from the development team behind BBC television's* Time Commanders.

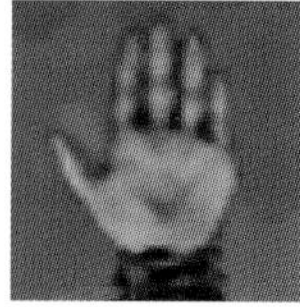

Several adjacent attractor points indicate the opportunity for versatile units, where it is possible for a unit positioned between the attractor points to function in several different strategic roles without being the optimum unit for any of them. This is a feature much appreciated by RTS gamers in particular, where there's rarely enough time to cherry-pick the perfect unit.

FROM CHIVALRY TO CYBERNETICS

How does all this apply to game design? It is game design! If you truly modelled a complete physics system, it would be impossible to define the ideal units – not because you couldn't identify the initial attractor points, but because they would change as the game was played. The heavy cavalry style of warfare that reaches its peak with the knight in full plate is soon obsolete once you introduce gunpowder weapons, and so on.

In practice, most wargames freeze the technology within pre-defined limits. Only a few, such as *Empire Earth*, purport to cover the changing face of warfare. Even then, the designers don't usually create a system that reflects how the nature of the balance shifts – how an attractor might move around the axes from defence to attack, for example. Instead, the overall pattern remains the same and effectively it's just the scale of the axes that changes. A starship trooper is a knight in servo-powered armour, only waiting for the laser upgrade that will spell his Agincourt.

WHATEVER HAPPENED TO THE RED SQUIRREL?

In general, designers try to avoid clustering multiple units around a single attractor point. For instance, there's not much point in having a dozen units that are functionally similar but differ by ten per cent in their armour and firepower balance. Why? Because it's wasted development effort to create them. One of those units is the fittest for the job and the others are non-optimal versions that, in a real ecosystem, would go the way of the dinosaurs. The ideal strategy game system would allow players to customise units based on an underlying economy. The underlying structures that manifest themselves as speed, armour and other attributes each have a cost. The economy changes as new technologies become available – e.g., new alloys reducing the cost of armour, hollow bones making flight more efficient, and so on. In such a game you would see the constant evolution of new strategies, very probably in ways the designers never anticipated. This is what makes the coming generation of Artificial Life based strategy games so promising.

All pictures: *Relic's* ***Impossible Creatures*** *allows players to create their own hybrids, resulting in a hugely diverse set of possible units to fight with.*

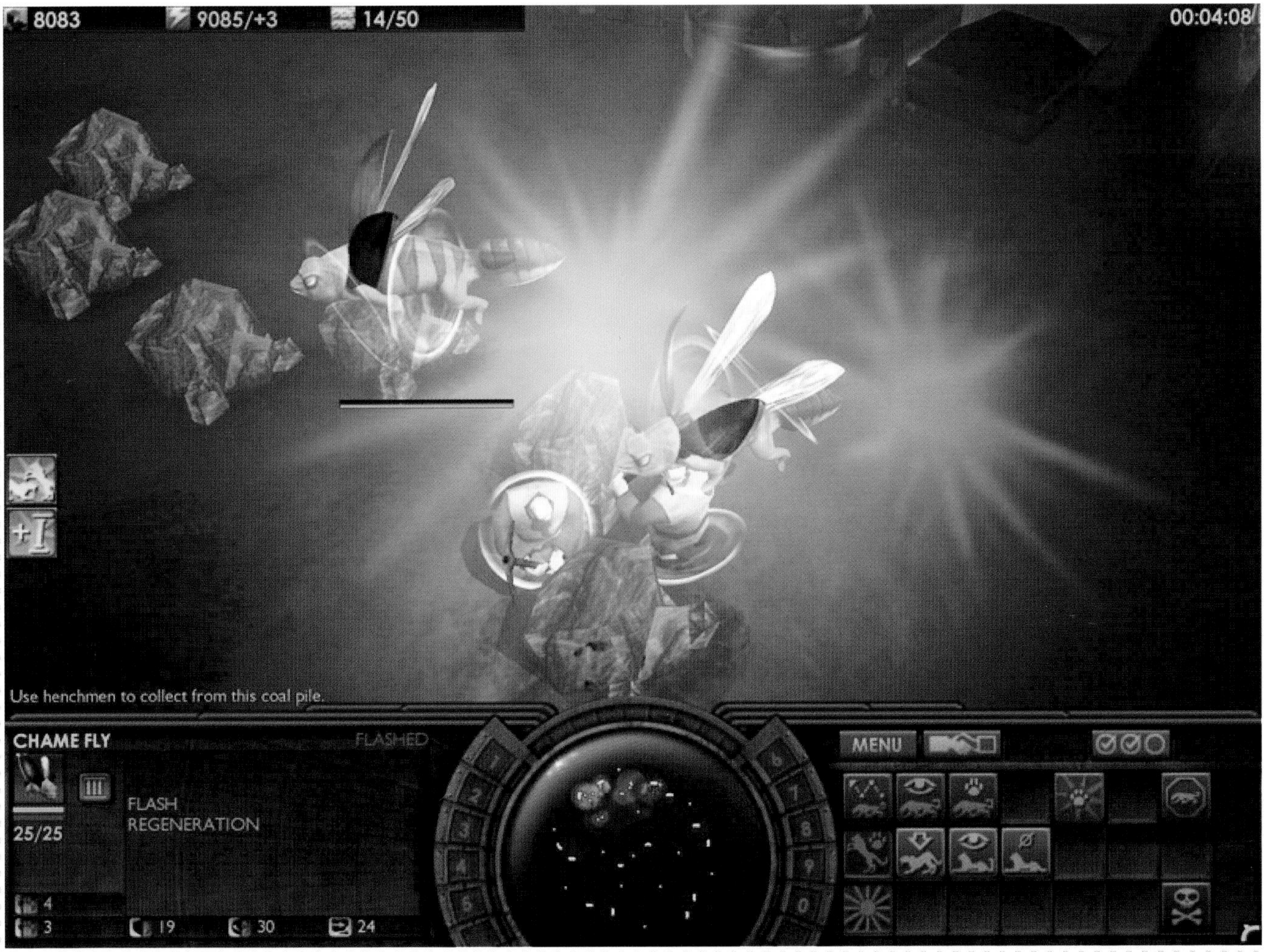

8083 9085/+3 14/50 00:04:08

Use henchmen to collect from this coal pile.

CHAME FLY
FLASHED
25/25
FLASH
REGENERATION
4
3
19
30
24
MENU

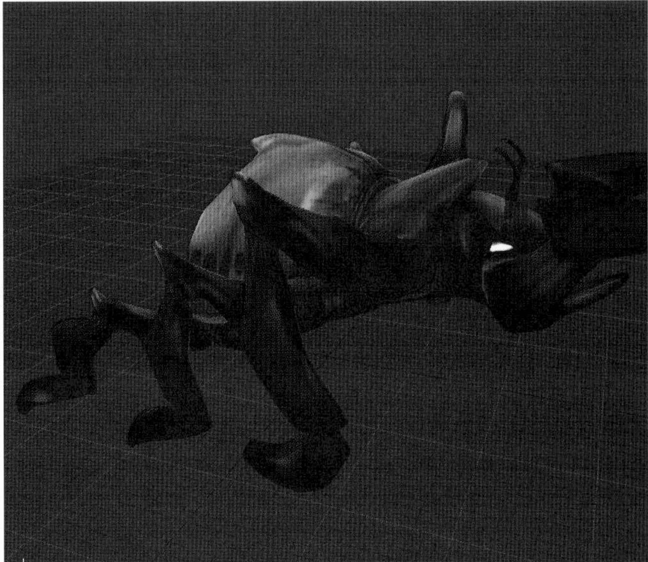

THE LIE OF THE LAND

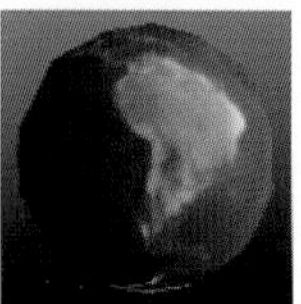

TERRAIN, WEATHER AND OTHER ENVIRONMENTAL FACTORS ALL CONTRIBUTE SIGNIFICANTLY TO STRATEGIC GAMEPLAY. IN REAL LIFE, GENERALS PLAN THEIR CAMPAIGNS TO AVOID THE WINTER; EXPLORERS USE THE OCEAN'S SEASONAL CURRENTS; TYCOONS WAIT UNTIL THE MARKET IS RIGHT.

KD Labs' game ***Perimeter*** *makes manipulating the terrain a strategic part of gameplay.*

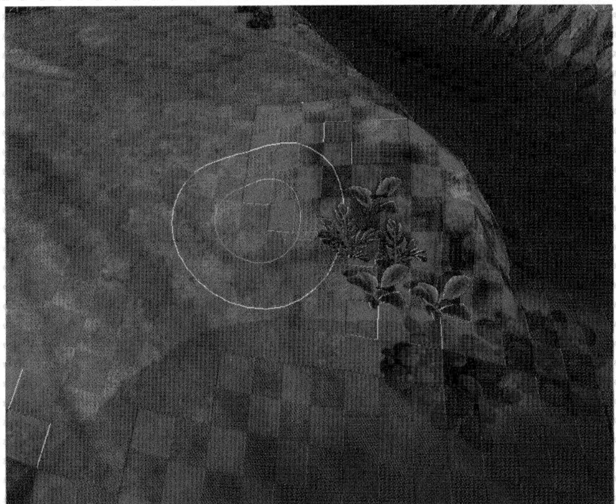

Left: ***Impossible Creatures*** *by Relic. Terrain in development. Islands make perfect battlegrounds because their restricted landmass makes it clear when a player has won.*

Without environmental factors to perturb the rules, all strategy games would reduce to chess: a problem with a finite range of solutions. There would be no possibility of simulating the opportunism of narrow ground that the English longbowmen exploited at Agincourt, or Yoshitsune's descent of the cliff at Ichi-no-tani, or Harold's defensive strategy at Hastings. Pikemen would always defeat spearmen and every battle would be a foregone conclusion. In reality, pikes require a closely ordered formation. Difficult terrain soon destabilises the phalanx, an interesting consideration that an enemy commander can make use of.

Early strategy games used 2D environments, and so designers still thought of them as boardgames with pretty graphics. Modern games model a full 3D environment in which environmental factors are inherent, enriching the gameplay possibilities. At the same time, 3D opens up a can of worms. Without flying units in a game, for example, much of the 3D space is unused. But if you do have flying units, you start to confront the player with extra headaches – the need to move the camera, to select units in the air, to spin around, to zoom in and out, and so on.

'FIGHT DOWNHILL; DO NOT ASCEND TO ATTACK.'

SUN TZU

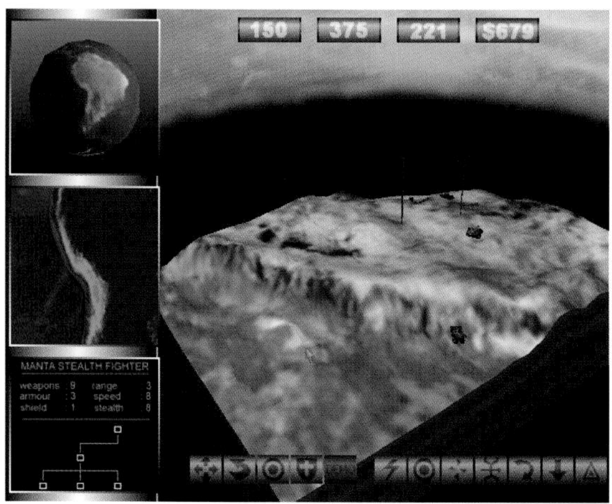

Left; *This screenshot from an early prototype of Eidos'* ***2020 Knife Edge****, programmed by Lee Briggs, shows one technique for depicting a flying unit's altitude using droplines. The colour of the drop-line could also be used to show other data such as whether the unit was fully fuelled, or whether ascending or descending, etc.*

Below: ***Republic: The Revolution*** *by Elixir Studios. Working in 3D gives more flexibility in production. For example, in the old days of 2D and isometrics, the angle of view had to be chosen on day one and then all art assets had to be created to follow that decision.*

With true 3D you can have characters being flung across the landscape, plunging down cliffs, and so on. It was not impossible to model such things in 2D, but only by clumsy artifice and never with the emergent possibilities that 3D allows.

THE LIE OF THE LAND 2

THE FREEDOM OF 3D

Today's strategy games are finding their own compromises. Ensemble's *Age of Mythology*, for example, is fully 3D but opts for a fixed high-angle view which is not so very different at first glance from the isometric view of earlier titles in the series. Blizzard's *Warcraft 3* allows players to rotate and tilt the view, although in practice most players settle on an angle that suits them and then get on with the game. Lionhead's *Black & White*, on the other hand, expects the player to change perspective constantly. An effective technique is to soar up into the clouds, swing around to the view you want, and then swoop back down to an intimate view. *Black & White's* gameplay is mostly more leisurely than you get in a straight RTS, so the extra control is feasible – as well as enhancing the player's sense of being a deity existing in a dimension beyond the mundane world.

It would be easy to exaggerate the problems of 3D, but to do so only betrays that the designer is still thinking of strategy as a two-dimensional boardgame-style genre. In most circumstances, camera AI can quite easily intuit what the player wants to look at. There will be occasions when the player might miss an approaching enemy legion hidden in the lee of a cliff – but is that a shortcoming, or is it an interesting artefact of the system? It was easy enough in 2D

Above: ***Stronghold* by** Firefly. *One of the most delightful offshoots of modern strategy game development is this kind of living representation of reality. A medieval smallholding is a thing of beauty in its own right – at least until the enemy armies arrive to raze it to the ground.*

Above: ***Homeworld 2*** by Relic. *Space strategy games came of age with the advent of 3D.*

to blank out areas that lay outside the player's line of sight, but the player was always aware of the blind spot. Now we have the possibility of genuine oversights. This is why 3D is richer – even if that richness sometimes creates frustrations, just as for the real-life military commander.

THE ROLE OF TERRAIN

Terrain can affect units' speed, range, survival and fighting ability. The interrelationship of these factors can lead to rewarding gameplay, but the designer must avoid making them too complex.

For example, consider a game with tanks, infantry, artillery and planes. We can see intuitively that you aren't going to want to get your tanks into marshland. Steep ridges will slow down the deployment of artillery. Planes can go anywhere regardless of terrain but they need airports nearby to return to. Infantry must carry their own supplies and so will be liable to attrition in barren ground where they are unable to forage.

All of those relationships are understood because they derive from the player's domain of experience. Now suppose the units are bionauts, plasma riders, vulanth hybrids and thanolasers. We have no guideline to tell us when we start the game that plasma riders are strong but cannot attack airborne units, or that bionauts can scale cliffs without loss of speed.

This is not to say that sci-fi or fantasy isn't a valid setting for strategy games, just that the combat paradigms are rarely intuitive and so it is harder to play such a game fluently – that is, without passing all decisions through the 'rules lawyer' part of the brain. This makes audacious and brilliant use of terrain much less likely.

Artificial intelligence in strategy games is an increasingly complex problem. 3D has made it much more difficult than in the old days of 2D. A designer could analyse a 2D map and represent it to the AI fairly easily. The extra dimension more than doubles the complexity. Computer opponents now need to analyse the attributes of a landscape and think of ways to use it to their advantage. Having fully deformable 3D landscapes is going to make it even more difficult. Over the next few pages we look at how designers are going to handle the problem.

HOW CAN WE CREATE GOOD AI FOR GAMES? THE IDEAL WOULD BE A COMPUTER OPPONENT THAT IS INDISTINGUISHABLE FROM ANOTHER HUMAN PLAYER IN CUNNING, AUDACITY, FORETHOUGHT, DIPLOMACY, AND EVEN IN ITS OCCASIONAL STUPIDITY. HENCE A TRULY EFFECTIVE AI FOR A STRATEGY GAME WOULD BE THE PUREST FORM OF THE TURING TEST, BASED NOT ON VERBAL COMMUNICATION BUT ON ACTION.

ARTIFICIAL OPPONENTS

It's easy enough to make a computer opponent who can win. The computer can act much faster than a human, giving it a distinct advantage in the routine elements of an RTS such as building and resource collecting. Given sufficient resources, even the dumbest military commander can gain victory.

WINNING WITH STYLE

But that doesn't make for a very satisfying game. The player wants an opponent with personality. He wants to be able to infer how the opponent might behave – but at the same time for it not to be totally predictable. If he loses, the player wants it to be because the AI used superior tactics, not because it cheated on resources and just kept pumping out troops.

Black Cactus's *Warrior Kings Battles* updated the idea used by Dave and Barry Murray in *The Ancient Art of War* of giving each opponent a personality. Some would remember a betrayal forever, others were more forgiving, and so on. This works well as long as there is enough randomness to prevent the opponent from becoming completely predictable. The results, although satisfying, are not always what the designer expected. In *Ancient Art of War*, Sun Tzu was supposed to be the hardest commander to beat. However, his habit of breaking off an attack on a beaten foe in order to try and march around to get at an unguarded flag meant that he could easily be suckered into a trap. The AI for Genghis Khan was ostensibly stupider. However, its relentless emphasis on destroying troops in the field made it, in a game where you couldn't step up resource production, the more fearsome foe.

***DANNY BELANGER*, Director of Internal Development at Strategy First, describes some of the factors to consider in designing convincing artificial intelligence:**
'Creating decision-making artificial intelligence gets difficult when you want to have the AI plan on multiple levels. AI is a lot more about what the player expects than the best strategy for the situation. Pathfinding is a good illustration of this. When the player clicks on a location, he wants the AI to use a path he sees on his screen. If the AI turns the unit around and goes another way, even if it is finding a better path, the player will be frustrated by the apparently unpredictable behaviour. The AI governing the player's own units must meet the player's demands and expectations.

Left and above: ***Chicago 1930*** *by Spellbound. Battlefield AI can become very complex, but character-driven AI has to deal with yet another set of variables.*

Above: ***The Ancient Art of War*** *lets you pick your opponent from the great commanders of history. Each had his own character and would fight in different ways.*

ARTIFICIAL OPPONENTS 2

MY TOWN CENTRE IS DAMAGED

IS THE TOWN CENTRE ON FIRE?

YES ASSIGN PEASANTS TO FIREFIGHTING

NO

ARE THERE ENEMY UNITS ATTACKING THE TOWN CENTRE?

YES ANALYSE TYPES AND NUMBERS OF ATTACKERS. ASSIGN UNITS TO COUNTER THEM. REFER TO ARMY COMPOSITION AND TASK PRIORITY FLOW-CHARTS

NO IS THE TOWN CENTRE STILL TAKING DAMAGE?

YES SEND OUT SCOUTS TO SWEEP AROUND CITY FOR HIDDEN ENEMY

NO

END – ASSIGN PEASANTS TO REPAIR DAMAGED TOWN CENTRE

'On the other hand, the AI opponent has the role of keeping the player busy and entertained as well as looking like it's intelligent. From my experience, this is where a lot of tricks or AI "cheats" are used to make the AI challenging from the beginning of the level to the end, since the computer opponent is not just there to try and win, but also to make the game interesting.'

SCRIPTS OR SMARTS?

In general, true AI solutions require development of a system that more or less understands a situation, to the level of being able to assess it and formulate a response on the fly. Scripted solutions are much simpler, comprising flow-charted checklists that the system works through to find a response:

As this example, a very simple AI flow-chart (opposite), shows, you would actually build a hierarchy of scripted routines to perform different functions. Army Composition (which chooses the right mix of units for a task) and Task Priority (which decides where to take those units from) are separate AI components that will be called on by various higher-level routines.

In a strategy game, at the highest level you might have a goal such as 'destroy the enemy city' and then an Army Commander AI might make demands on the Treasurer AI for allocation of resources to build an army, then delegate choice of operational and tactical objectives to General and Battalion Commander AIs respectively – right on down to the routines that tell each soldier where to move and who to shoot at.

Neural nets, on the other hand, are systems built of layers of intercommunicating nodes that can change the weighting between their various inputs and outputs. The neural net can learn to recognise patterns. You present the top layer with an input that may be quite complex – a signature, a photograph, etc. – and then adjust the bottom layer's output in order to train the network. The output for the signature could be whether it is real or a forgery. The output for the photograph might be whether it's of a man or woman, and so on.

Neural nets are good at this kind of abstraction from the specific to the symbols beneath the surface. For example, it's possible to train neural nets to recognise gender from faces more accurately than humans can. In our own brains we build networks of nets. You can feel that most obviously when you see something and respond intuitively, without really needing to think. Great army commanders no doubt had that kind of intuitive grasp of tactical problems. We all do it constantly when we look at instances of objects – a cup, a dustbin, a box, a tray, a jar, etc. – and are able to recognise all of these as types of container.

That's just the same kind of thing we're doing when playing a game we're good at. Hence in theory it should be possible to use neural nets to recognise levels of threat – the size and type of an opponent's approaching army, for example – and return appropriate strategies.

Disciples II: Dark Prophecy *by Strategy First. AI has to be cleverer at squad level than at a larger strategic scale with hundreds of units, because the player is more focused on the behaviour of individual units.*

IS Games' **War Times**. The artificial intelligence in a strategy game should be smart enough to see that if its first wave gets destroyed, there's no point carrying out the same attack all over again. It should never reinforce failure.

Flowchart-based AIs return the same solution every time. To avoid this, the designer needs to build in the capacity for the flow-chart to 'remember' previous defeats and, if not learn from them, at least try a new tack next time.

ARTIFICIAL OPPONENTS 3

THE GHOST IN THE MACHINE

One drawback is that neural nets learn quickly but they're 'lazy' – they'll spot the obvious pattern, but that pattern may serve to conceal something more complex underneath. When the US Army was training neural nets to select aerial photographs showing camouflaged tanks, it got a 90% level of accuracy on early tests, and then suddenly found the same neural nets getting it wrong. Researchers were mystified until they realised that the original photos used to train the nets had been taken on different days. All the photos showing concealed tanks were taken on a sunny day, all the ones without tanks on the next day, which was overcast. The neural net had just learned to tell when the sun was shining!

Obviously an oversight like that could easily be exploited by a human player. It needn't be something that would be immediately obvious in testing. For example, the AI designer might inadvertently train the neural net to respond to close clusters of enemy units, rather than to the genuine scale of threat, so sneaking a hundred men up to the walls one by one might go unnoticed.

That also illustrates the other drawback. You can't easily crack into a neural net and ask why it's returning a given result. You can't ask it in the way you could ask a scripted system which part of the flow-chart it was getting stuck on. Neural nets distribute the whole process of turning one pattern into another within their layers of connections. They may not even learn the same way twice – all of which makes them interesting to AI researchers but a real headache for game developers.

Top: ***1503 AD: The New World*** *by Sunflowers.*

Above & left: *Sid Meier's* ***Alpha Centauri*** *from Firaxis.*

'EVERYTHING WHICH THE ENEMY LEAST EXPECTS WILL SUCCEED THE BEST.'

FREDERICK THE GREAT

ARTIFICIAL OPPONENTS 5

THINKING BY NUMBERS

Script-based systems are simpler but have their drawbacks, too. Most obviously, they are highly predictable. Forewarned is forearmed, as they say – which means that if you can work out what your opponent is going to do in response to any action, you have a distinct edge.

A very common example of this is the trigger point. These are familiar features in virtually any RTS. You advance to a river crossing and the enemy surge toward you. You retreat, they pursue a little way and then go back to their side of the river. So you probe a few more times to find exactly where the trigger point is, then you take time to build up an overwhelming force just beyond the trigger – before charging in to annihilate the stupid computer opponent, who didn't even have the sense to reinforce.

There are solutions to that. The designer can create a virtual scout unit in place of a fixed trigger point. The virtual unit (which you can't see) has its own AI. Maybe it ventures over to the other side of the river when its player is strong, but if he's currently rebuilding his army after another battle it draws back closer to its home city. It could also observe enemy forces massing nearby and send warnings back to its own Army Commander AI to reinforce. Building some randomness – or even just a cyclical path – into the virtual unit's patrol area helps to make it look unpredictable from the human player's viewpoint.

This all adds to the messages flying around, of course – which matters less than it used to, as processing power continues to increase. But even now that the machines can handle it, there is still a cost in design time.

Top: *Codo International's* ***Laser Squad Nemesis.***

Above: *Firefly's* ***Stronghold.***

Right: ***Space Colony*** *by Firefly.*

4033
00:00 Day 12

THE MAIN CHANCE

IN SECURING VICTORY, TIMING IS EVERYTHING. NAPOLEON SAID: 'STRATEGY IS THE ART OF MAKING USE OF TIME AND SPACE. I AM LESS CONCERNED ABOUT THE LATTER. SPACE WE CAN RECOVER; LOST TIME NEVER.'

'OPPORTUNITY IN WAR IS USUALLY OF GREATER VALUE THAN BRAVERY . . . TERRAIN IS OFTEN OF MORE VALUE THAN BRAVERY . . . BRAVERY IS OF MORE VALUE THAN NUMBERS.'
VEGETIUS

Left & right: *Digital Reality's* ***Haegemonia.***

Below: ***Evil Genius*** *from Elixir Studios.*

The best strategy games are designed to highlight emergent, transient factors that reward vigilance on the part of the players.

Suppose that the game has weather, seasons and a day/night cycle – the latter admittedly rather annoying when implemented in the context of a strategy game, but this is only an illustration. After playing for a while, I realise that my policy of mainly building cavalry is looking like a disaster given that my opponent has hundreds of musketeers drilled to fight in tight squares. But just then, night-time coincides with heavy winter rains. Conditions are now on my side. I can move in with an all-cavalry army, which is swift enough not to suffer winter attrition as it crosses the plain between our cities. Night attacks favour cavalry (remember, the horses can see), while the rain is going to turn all those muskets into damp squibs.

It's unlikely that any real-time game would actually strive for quite that level of complexity, but the lesson is clear. A game that allows for changing conditions – even if they change predictably – provides the means to break a deadlock between players. The player with an eye for the main chance will prevail. These are the kind of games that provide us with the 'surprise and delight' factor.

'ALTHOUGH THERE HAVE BEEN INSTANCES OF FOOLISH HASTE IN WAR, CLEVERNESS HAS NEVER BEEN ASSOCIATED WITH LONG DELAY.' SUN TZU

'VICTORY LIES IN THE ART OF CONCENTRATING STRENGTH AT A POINT, FORCING A BREAKTHROUGH, ROLLING UP AND SECURING THE FLANKS ON BOTH SIDES, AND THEN DRIVING LIKE LIGHTNING FAR INTO THE ENEMY'S REAR BEFORE HE HAS TIME TO REACT.'

ERWIN ROMMEL

THE MAIN CHANCE 2

Above: ***Desperados 2*** *by Spellbound.*

Left: *The hole in the wall gang strike again in Firefly's* ***Stronghold.***

Opportunistic play of this kind need not only arise from changing environmental conditions, however. Another source is the unforeseen exploitation of a set of rules that, acting together, create an effect that is not immediately anticipated. (By the way, this is not the same thing as the much over-used term 'emergence', which describes an outcome that cannot be predicted by purely theoretical means.)

Unforeseen rules effects can be illustrated by Lanchester's Second (or N-squared) Law, which states that the relative strength of two bodies of men armed with missile weapons is in proportion to the squares of their sizes. If 1000 archers attack 500, you can see that only one quarter of the larger force will be lost in the time it takes to destroy the smaller force. This result applies to missile units but not to shock (melée) troops. This is incidentally one of the reasons why missile units were disproportionately effective in early RTS games such as *Age of Empires*. Real-time abandoned the authentic limitations on missile troops – namely, that they are often inaccurate and prone to run out of ammunition. In the absence of those rules, missiles became much more effective than shock troops – the reverse of true experience in ancient warfare.

The most famous example of Lanchester's N-squared Law in operation was at Trafalgar. Admiral Nelson with only 27 ships was outnumbered by the French, who had 33 ships, but he seized an opportunity to attack 23 ships of the enemy fleet while the remaining ten ships tacked around to return and engage him. By the time the second French force was in a position to fire, Nelson had shattered the first group and had 13 vessels still fully operational. He then crippled the remaining French force with eight ships to spare – precisely as F. W. Lanchester would have predicted, though admittedly his analysis came a century on from Nelson's more intuitive use of the rule.

'IN WAR, THE SLOWER THE ACTION PROCEEDS, THE MORE FREQUENT AND LONGER THE PERIODS OF INACTIVITY, AND SO ERRORS CAN BE CORRECTED MORE EASILY. THEREFORE, THE COMMANDER CAN BE BOLDER IN HIS DECISIONS ... [AND] ... DEPENDING ON WHETHER THE COURSE OF THE WAR IS FASTER OR SLOWER, MORE OR LESS TIME WILL BE AVAILABLE FOR THE CALCULATION OF PROBABILITIES BASED ON THE GIVEN CIRCUMSTANCES.'

CARL VON CLAUSEWITZ, ON WAR

REAL-TIME OR TURN-BASED?

In the real-time vs. turn-based debate, Clausewitz seems to come down on the side of the latter. The serious student of war usually prefers to take his time over decisions. When a time limit is applied in tabletop wargaming tournaments, it's typically quite leisurely. The goal – as the grand strategist sees it – is to conduct war as you might a croquet match, delivering brutality with a languid smile and showing only the tips of the teeth.

Not for those old-school gamers the feral, heart-pounding cut and thrust of a modern RTS. When decisions must be made in the heat of the moment, it's easy to overlook things. Mistakes often carry a harsh price.

The purist argument is that real time dissipates the strategy. The game becomes a question also of reaction speed, multi-tasking, daring, and the ability to keep cool under pressure.

Those are not strictly the qualities of a strategist, but they are essential to any real-life commander. They comprise what Clausewitz calls 'the genius for war' and are essential to the execution of strategy whether that war involves gunpowder volleys across a muddy field, or hostile takeovers across a mahogany boardroom table.

A halfway house is emerging between these two camps – the game that goes into bullet time (slow motion) while players are entering new orders, but then goes to real time to display the results. Such a game encourages thoughtful construction of overall strategies with the possibility of fine-tuning in the thick of battle. *2020 Knife Edge*, for example, was a game in development at Eidos in the late 1990s.

Players assembled hierarchies of units and were able to pre-set 'orchestral' defensive and attacking protocols during the slower phase of the game; the units then carried out those protocols in real time.

Real-time gaming has blown the dust off the strategy genre. The risk is that it can reduce the game experience to thoughtless mouse-clicking – which is a perfectly respectable pastime, but not what strategy fans are interested in. The goal is a game that is simple enough to allow players to grasp a situation intuitively and formulate strategies, and with an interface that allows them to enact those strategies fluently.

Below: ***Laser Squad: Nemesis*** *by Codo International. Turn-based games allow for leisurely sessions played over email. The time between turns gives players the opportunity to ponder their moves.*

Inset: *The genesis of* ***Laser Squad****: the seminal* ***Rebelstar Raiders*** *on the 8-bit ZX Spectrum.*

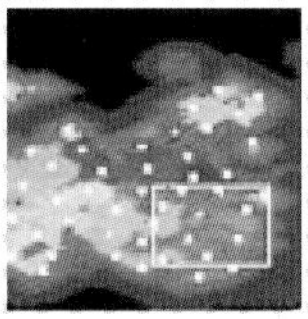

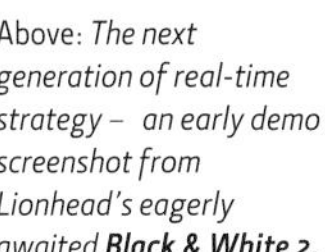

Above: *The next generation of real-time strategy – an early demo screenshot from Lionhead's eagerly awaited* ***Black & White 2.***

EACH STRATEGY GAME FINDS ITS OWN BALANCE BETWEEN MOBILITY AND STABILITY, WHICH IN THE SPECIFIC CASE OF THE MILITARY GAME IS THE TRADE-OFF BETWEEN ATTACK AND DEFENCE.

The ***2020 Knife Edge*** *design allowed players to create hierarchies of units and pre-set their behaviour protocols, allowing complex battle plans to be prepared for both attack and defence. In effect, the player wrote the 'orchestral' battle plans and then only had to fine-tune them with orders to specific units once the fighting began.*

Historically the balance has seesawed – from the virtual impregnability of medieval castles to the superiority of attack in the Napoleonic era to the stagnant trench warfare of World War 1 and back to the blitzkrieg of the later 20th century.

The designer of real-time strategy games not only has to consider the relative strengths of attack and defence embodied in the rules, but also the ease of use by the player. In most RTS games it is far simpler to set up a pattern of walls, towers and forts and be able to rely on them to work as expected, than it is to coordinate a mixture of troops on the attack.

Below: ***Robin Hood: The Legend of Sherwood*** by *Spellbound*.

You also need to bear in mind that missile troops have an effectiveness in proportion to the square of the ratio of numbers, whereas in the case of shock troops the relationship is linear. Since towers and laser turrets are customarily ranged units, this again makes them much more effective than the firepower strengths written into the game code might suggest.

Creating defences is a lot of fun. Players enjoy building things – and they don't come much better than a physical structure that inspires a creator's pride and also delights the tactician's eye by being a three-dimensional depiction of a defensive battle plan. On top of that, strategy gamers (on the PC at any rate, and it can be argued there are no true strategy games on console) tend to be planners rather than on-the-fly thinkers. They enjoy the ability to 'programme' their battle plans, even via the imprecise medium of mere physical placement.

A game that becomes bogged down in defence soon becomes tedious. If neither side can break a deadlock, you enter the devil's arithmetic of the trenches where a million men die to gain a mile of ground. To prevent stalemate, designers need to remember the inherent benefits of defence and to counter these by limiting defensive strength. Weaker walls are good, but stronger artillery that works specifically against walls and fortifications is better – partly because specialised unit functions create more interesting gameplay, but also because you can build in early availability of walls and later upgrades for artillery to ensure that players have time to build up in the early phases of the game before war starts to shatter those elegant cities.

If the designer builds in a changing dynamic between attack and defence, this helps stimulate the classic pattern of the strategy wargame: establish, explore, compete, defend and conquer.

'FIXED FORTIFICATIONS ARE MONUMENTS TO THE STUPIDITY OF MAN.'

GEORGE PATTON

SECTION

PEACE 2

WAR IS NOT, OF COURSE, THE ENTIRETY OF THE STRATEGY GENRE. ANDREW ROLLINGS AND ERNEST ADAMS, IN THEIR BOOK ON GAME DESIGN, IDENTIFIED THREE BASIC ACTIVITIES THAT COMPRISE THE CORE OF MOST STRATEGY GAMES. THESE ARE: CONQUEST, EXPLORATION AND COMMERCE.

MOST STRATEGY GAMES UTILISE ALL THREE, THE SPECIFIC MIX DEFINING THE FLAVOUR OF THE GAME. EVEN IN THE MOST COMBAT-ORIENTED GAME, THERE MUST BE OTHER ELEMENTS OR IT IS NOT STRATEGY. A GAME IN WHICH PLAYERS EACH TAKE A PRE-DEFINED ARMY AND FIGHT ONLY WITH THOSE UNITS WOULD – IN THE ABSENCE OF RULES CATERING FOR ECONOMY, BUILDING, OR HIDDEN MOVEMENT – BE ONLY TACTICS, NOT STRATEGY.

WHEN ALL CONQUEST ELEMENTS ARE STRIPPED AWAY, THE STRATEGY GENRE TENDS TOWARDS MANAGEMENT. STILL IN THE REALM OF TRUE STRATEGY WE HAVE TITLES SUCH AS **REPUBLIC: THE REVOLUTION** AND **STARTOPIA**. AS THE SLIDER MOVES TOWARDS MANAGEMENT WE MAY START TO CONSIDER **ROLLERCOASTER TYCOON**, **HOTEL GIANT**, AND EVEN **THE SIMS**.

ARE THESE DIVISIONS MEANINGFUL? AS WE DISCUSSED AT THE START, A STRATEGY IS A BASIS FOR MAKING DECISIONS THROUGHOUT THE GAME – A PHILOSOPHY OF ACTION, IN OTHER WORDS. BY CONTRAST, PURE MANAGEMENT GAMES OFTEN REDUCE TO A SYSTEM OF INTERDEPENDENT PARTS THAT THE PLAYER MUST ADJUST TO BRING THE SYSTEM TO EQUILIBRIUM. OFTEN THERE IS ONLY ONE EQUILIBRIUM AND A SMALL NUMBER OF PATHS TO REACH THAT POINT. ONCE THE PLAYER HAS A GOOD GRASP OF THE 'SPRINGS' LINKING THE SYSTEM, THE SOLUTION IS MORE A MATTER OF PATIENCE THAN INNOVATIVE THOUGHT.

THE ANALYSIS IS ONLY FOR THEORISTS, AND GENRES MATTER MORE TO MARKETERS THAN TO CONSUMERS. AS GAMERS, ALL WE ARE CONCERNED ABOUT IS HAVING FUN!

1503 AD: The New World *from Sunflowers.*

resources

*The magnificent panoply of war: **Age of Mythology** from Ensemble Studios is the ultimate tabletop gamer's dream.*

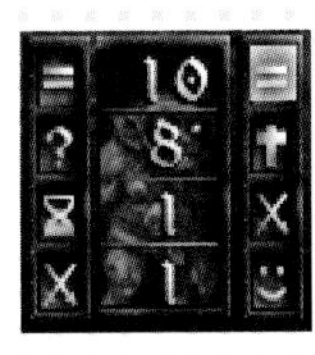

A FAMOUS OLD ENGLISH PUB IN DEVON, THE FOUR ALLS, BEARS A QUARTERED SIGN SHOWING A MONARCH, A KNIGHT, A BISHOP AND A PEASANT. THE UNSTATED CAPTIONS ARE: 'I RULE ALL', 'I FIGHT FOR ALL', 'I PRAY FOR ALL' AND 'I WORK FOR ALL'. THE LAST IS A PRETTY GOOD SUMMARY OF THE CORE ECONOMIC MOTOR OF MOST STRATEGY GAMES.

The peasant may go by other names. Depending on the game setting he can be a spice harvester, robot, miner, imp, or nanomachine. His function, however, is always the same – to build the infrastructure that sustains your army, and to gather the resources to fuel that infrastructure.

The strategy genre is often thought of as synonymous with wargaming, but the fact is that conflict in such games is only one part of the process of empire-building. In games, as in life, everything is driven by the competition for resources.

Without resources, in fact, a game cannot be said to involve strategy. I could design a wargame in which each player selected troops bought using a points system at the start of battle. Such a game would require tactics – that is, the deployment and use of different troop types. But it would not involve strategy. Strategy deals with the planning of objectives, logistics and reinforcement, which become irrelevant if there is no underlying economic resource.

***CHARLIE BEWSHER* of Black Cactus Games explains the way resources fit into gameplay:**

'The economy in a real-time strategy game acts as a catalyst for emergent gameplay. It affects the game at three levels. First it offers the player a fundamental strategic choice. Do I invest in my economy or my military? Do I boom or rush? This conflict is essential in pacing RTS games.

'Second it gives the game world context – areas to defend, areas to target. It enables the players to create their own missions and strategies. Do I grab those far-off resources or will I be overreaching myself?

'Third it allows the players' personalities to come into the game world through how they spend the resources. Whether on defence or attack, heavy or light combat units, and so on. The players define how they will tackle the challenge.

'The number of resource types depends on the pacing and the focus of the game. Is it a fighting 'clickfest' or a grand strategy game? Standard economic bureaucracy – that is, not caused by enemy behaviour – should fill in non-fighting time to the extent that the player is stretched but never very distracted from the fighting.'

'IN STRATEGY WARGAMES, 90 PER CENT OF THE OUTCOME IS BASED ON YOUR RESOURCE-GATHERING STRATEGY. THE RESULT OF THE BATTLE IS DETERMINED BY THE TROOPS YOU'RE ABLE TO BUILD, WHICH COMES MORE FROM THE RESOURCE DOMAIN THAN THE MILITARY DOMAIN.' **IGNACIO PÉREZ,** DIRECTOR AT PYRO STUDIOS

TYPES OF RESOURCES

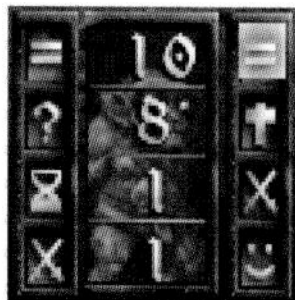

*Different resources in **Age of Mythology.***

Greek villagers continually harvest divine Favor, which goes directly to your resource stocks. The more villagers you have praying, the faster they generate Favor.

HARVESTED RESOURCES

Harvesting – the term derives from the collection of tiberium in *Command & Conquer* – requires your worker units to gather resources. The usual pattern is for the worker to go to the tree, gold mine, tiberium deposit, and so on. He works for a time and collects his carrying limit in resource points. He then has to return to a resource deposit point (timber yard, foundry, etc.) and drops off the collected resources, which in most games are then added to your global stocks.

The worker unit that does the harvesting can consist of specialists (collects only that specific resource) or generalists (can collect any resources). Specialised harvesters don't create very interesting game choices. The unit probably counts against a population limit, so you have to decide whether to build a harvester or another kind of unit, but that's all. The imps in *Dungeon Keeper*, on the other hand, need to be used for other tasks – not just harvesting gold, but tunnelling new rooms, claiming territory, collecting bodies and captives and reinforcing the dungeon walls.

When the harvester unit can also be used in battle, the player is faced with more game decisions. This applies to some of the Norse worker units in *Age of Mythology*, for example. For the true strategy aficionado, having more options is usually taken to be better, but in this instance the trade-off needs to be carefully thought through or else it becomes clutter. There may be more choices – but are they challenging choices? Since harvester units are weak in combat the player will only use them in a dire emergency: in other words, when there's no real choice. And making the harvester strong in combat is no solution, because you don't want a unit that is both versatile and powerful. That's no kind of trade-off.

Above left: *Villagers harvest wood by going to a forest and collecting it. There is a period of non-productive 'dead time' in every villager's work cycle as he carries wood back to the storage depot.*

Left: *Favor for the Norse player uses a less typical paradigm. Success in battle generates Favor. The better troop types require Favor to build, making this a positive feedback system: once the Norse start losing, they keep losing.*

Above: *The Egyptians use a different system. Favor is generated by monuments to the god. It doesn't require villagers, freeing them to do other work. The downside is that you can't increase the fixed rate at which Favor is generated.*

TYPES OF RESOURCES 2

Far left: *Of course, it's essential to protect your resources...*

Left: *...and man needs sustenance for the soul as well.*

Below: *But without all those workers in the fields, your power would be built on sand.*

SELF-GENERATING RESOURCES

Electricity in *Total Annihilation* doesn't need to be collected by workers. You just build the right structure and it flows in. (Solar collectors produce it at a slow but dependable rate; wind generators are more variable but produce more on average – an elegant little bit of design.)

From the player's point of view, self-generating resources are better than harvested resources. You don't have to do any micromanagement – looking for idle peasants who have finished a task, moving groups of them around to new resource points, and so on. The drawback is that you lose flexibility – you can't rapidly adjust the rate at which you're harvesting different resources; although you could if there's a building type that can be switched to generate various different resources. That requires some ingenuity in the game setting to justify it, however.

'IF STRATEGY GAMES DEALT WITH WARFARE ALONE, THE GAMEPLAY WOULD NOT BE AS CHALLENGING. JUST AS SUPPLY LINES ARE IMPORTANT IN WARFARE, RESOURCES SYMBOLISE THE IMPORTANCE NOT ONLY OF FIGHTING, BUT ALSO OF MAINTAINING YOUR ARMY. RESOURCES GIVE THE PLAYER AN INCENTIVE TO HAVE SOMETHING TO BUILD A DEFENSIVE STRATEGY AROUND.' **FREDRIK LINDGREN** OF PARADOX ENTERTAINMENT

Above: *Agriculture – the bedrock of all economies, in this instance it supports the people of Lionhead's* ***Black & White****.*

LOCALISED RESOURCES

In most strategy games, resources once collected become part of a global stock that exists outside the immediate game environment. This means that another player can't capture those resources even if he destroys his opponent's town. This can be very frustrating if it drags out the endgame. For instance, I might destroy all your forces apart from a single worker, who I then have to scour the map to find before he uses your ineluctable stocks of metal and deuterium to rebuild your army.

Black & White is one of the few where resources remain physically located in the world. Timber and grain are kept at your town hall and can be seized by enemy players. Since you actually get to stick your godlike hand in there and grab the resources like a pirate on a plunder frenzy, it really is rather satisfying, too. Localisation of resources is obviously more realistic. Not that realism is *de rigueur* in games by any means, but an element of realism does ensure that the player's expectations of good strategy are in line with what works in the game.

TYPES OF RESOURCES 3

EXHAUSTIBLE/INEXHAUSTIBLE RESOURCES

The resource in Bullfrog's *Dungeon Keeper* is gold, which can be harvested from two sources. First off there are seams of gold, which your imps will dig out and transfer as bags of gold to your treasure room. Also there are gem outcroppings. The advantage of gems is that they never run out, unlike gold seams. Your imps keep chipping away harvesting unlimited gold. The disadvantage is that the gold yield from gems is very slow.

The trade-off between exhaustible and inexhaustible resources can be seen in many games, although rarely with an interesting trade-off like the one in *Dungeon Keeper*. In *Age of Mythology*, for example, food is unlimited because once you have built farms you can go on producing food forever. But once all the trees are gone, like the inhabitants of Easter Island, you don't have any way of getting more wood. (Actually you do, because you can buy it at the market, but in practice the game never gets to that level of desperation.)

Dungeon Keeper had just one resource (treasure) with two different sources. If a game is going to feature multiple resources, some of which are inexhaustible, then they need to be used for different purposes. The weaker units should require only inexhaustible resources, for example, while the exhaustible resources should be used to build stronger units or those with special abilities. This encourages a cyclical flow to the game, wherein players will gather up stocks of the exhaustible resources and then use them to build forces for a big push.

It could be interesting, too, to include renewable resources. For example, trees could grow back at a rate proportional to the number of trees in an area. The players then have the choice whether to exhaust their local resources or go for a longer game in which they follow strategies that consume resources at a sustainable rate.

Above: *Greed is good in Bullfrog's* ***Dungeon Keeper.***

Right: *In the* ***Civilization*** *series by Firaxis, resources are inexhaustible.*

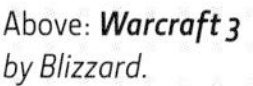

Above: ***Warcraft 3*** *by Blizzard.*

SHADOW RESOURCES

You can find some gems of design in the early RTS games. Take the original *Warcraft*. It is not immediately obvious that this game actually includes a shadow resource – namely food.

The way it works is this. To sustain your units you need to build farms. Possibly the designers originally had in mind that farms would produce food, and each unit would consume food to stay alive. But actually going to all the trouble of adding the food to the player's stocks only to have it trickle away as it was consumed is a needless complication. If we say that each character needs one food point per unit time, we can dispense with recording food altogether. We can just say (as *Warcraft*'s designers did) that you need to build one farm for every so many units.

q

TYPES OF RESOURCES

There are a number of different resource types in Firefly's ***Stronghold****, all combining to create a detailed interdependent economy. Indeed, the game gives the player the option of a purely economic victory condition. All resources have to go through at least one level of refinement – before wheat can be used it has to go to the bakers to be turned into bread, and so on. Perhaps the most interesting derived resource is happiness. With it, citizens work harder and are less likely to cause trouble. Happiness comes from the production system (most notably the brewing of hops into beer) and simple purchases such as maypoles and gardens, and is spent doing construction work and converted into money via taxes. Happiness is depicted by the expression of a scribe in the lower right of the interface, often found grinning even in defeat!*

Later RTS games kept the population limit effect but seem to have overlooked the reasoning. In *Age of Empires*, for example, you need one house for every five people in your population. But you also have to harvest food from farms. The food isn't used to sustain your characters because *Age of Empire's* designers rightly saw that having to juggle an ongoing and not very visible drain on a resource would not make for a fun game. Instead, you use food only when spawning units. But the fact remains that they have retained *Warcraft's* clever device of having food as a shadow resource – only now it's been reimagined as essential for growth.

STORAGE OF RESOURCES

It used to be quite common in early RTS games like *Command & Conquer* or *Total Annihilation* to cap the player's resource stocks depending on the number of storage silos he had built. When your resource stocks hit the cap, you needed to build more silos. Usually a player didn't lose resources if a silo was destroyed – although in some games he did, effectively making those resources 'weakly localised'.

Today most games have abandoned silos, making resource stocks limitless. There are still a few instances of caps: for example, in *Age of Mythology* you cannot store more than 100 points of divine Favor. But even there the system has been vastly simplified – you don't get the opportunity to build extra silos, the 100 Favor cap is an absolute limit.

Where the emphasis is still on the city-building aspect of the game – as in *Stronghold*, for instance – the storage limit has been retained. However, modern RTS games have moved away from this towards a purer representation of warfare. There, building the city is really just the process of building a visual interface for upgrades and unit-spawning. For this reason, RTS is de-emphasising the management of underlying economic factors and moving more towards abstraction at that level.

THERE IS AN OLD STORY ABOUT JAPAN GOING TO WAR WITH CHINA. ON THE FIRST DAY, THE CHINESE GENERAL TOLD HIS EMPEROR THAT THE JAPANESE HAD LOST 50 SOLDIERS AND THE CHINESE HAD LOST 500. ON THE NEXT DAY, THE JAPANESE LOST 1000 SOLDIERS AND THE CHINESE LOST 10,000. ON THE THIRD DAY, THE GENERAL REPORTED THAT THE JAPANESE LOSSES WERE 50,000 WHILE THE CHINESE LOST HALF A MILLION.

'WE'RE DOING TERRIBLY,' SAID THE EMPEROR. ***'SO WHY ARE YOU STILL SMILING?'***

'IT'S SIMPLE, YOUR MAJESTY,' SAID THE GENERAL.. ***'PRETTY SOON, NO JAPANESE.'***

THE BALANCE SHEET OF WARFARE

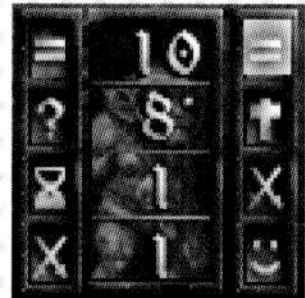

Resources are often less visible than the units in a game, so it is not always obvious at first glance how important the economy is. Your opponent might be a terrible commander and his military units could be only half as effective as yours. On the surface he might look like a loser – until, that is, you notice the scores clocking up in his resource counters at the top of the screen. If it turns out his economy is capable of pumping out units more than twice as fast as you, he's going to win.

Clausewitz said that the objective of war is to remove the enemy's ability to wage war. This involves first destroying the enemy's units in the field, and second interrupting the economic machinery that spawns new units.

In many wargames, the battle rules are well developed and allow for interesting gameplay. Very often, though, the economic aspect of the game is simply a question of racing to collect the limited resources before the other players do. Especially in wargames that favour defensive strategies, it's possible for the less deserving player to hold on long enough to purchase victory instead of earning it.

Of course, it's up to the other players to disrupt the hoarder's economy before he gets that powerful. After all, resources are usually a function of territory held, so if two skilled players are so busy fighting each other that they leave territory unguarded and so overlook the unskilled player who is meanwhile seizing all those resources, they only have themselves to blame.

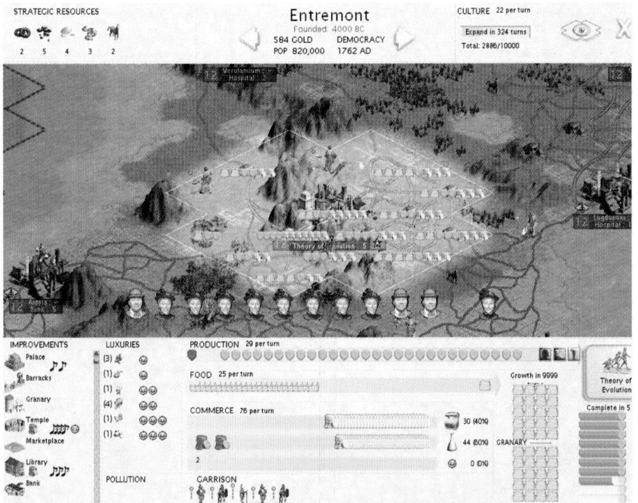

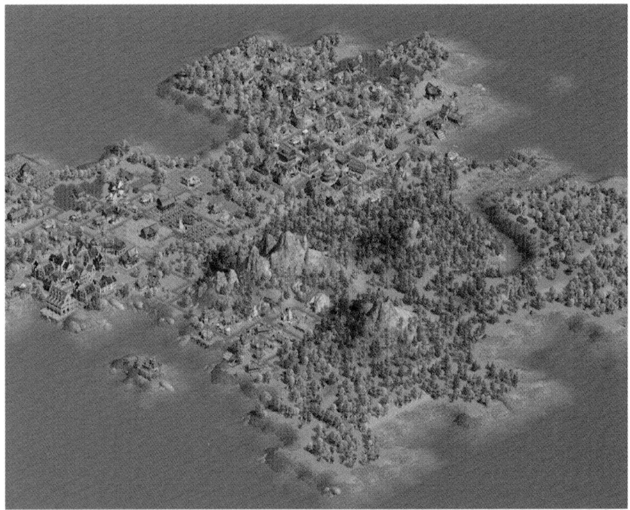

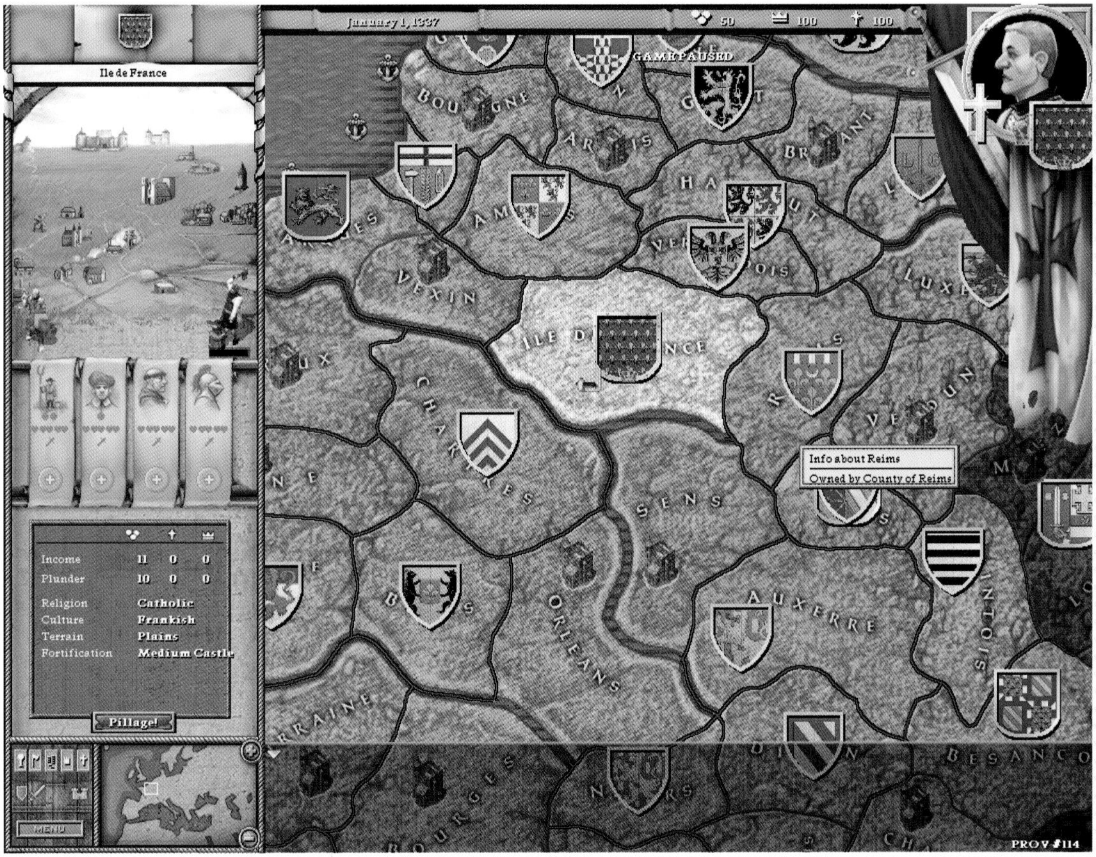

Above left: *The classic all-night strategy blockbuster:* ***Civilization 3*** *by Firaxis.*

Above: ***1503 AD: The New World*** *by Sunflowers.*

Left: Carving up the land of France in ***Crusader Kings*** *from Paradox.*

Far left: ***Dungeon Keeper 2*** *from Bullfrog shows how it's easier for players to remember the value of resources when they are not tallied off-screen but are physically represented within the game environment, even after being collected. You can see and almost feel those straining sacks of gold in* ***Dungeon Keeper****, the piles of grain and wood in* ***Black & White*** *and the stacks of coins in* ***Civilization****. This is far preferable to having resources shown as an abstract counter value – a carry-over from the genre's origins in boardgaming.*

HOME

BUILDING A BASE FULFILS SEVERAL FUNCTIONS IN STRATEGY GAMING. FIRST AND MOST OBVIOUSLY, A BASE IS A THING TO DEFEND. THREATS TO YOUR CITY FUEL THE MOTOR OF THE GAME, WHETHER THOSE THREATS ARE FROM EXTERNAL CONQUERORS OR INTERNAL PROBLEMS SUCH AS REBELLION, POVERTY, DISEASE OR DISASTER. THE FLIPSIDE IS THAT IT PROVIDES A CLEAR WAY TO DELINEATE THE ENDGAME. IF BUILDING YOUR BASE WAS THE BEGINNING, AND SUSTAINING AND NURTURING AND PROTECTING IT WAS THE MIDDLE, THEN WATCHING IT COLLAPSE IN FLAMES IS AN INCONTROVERTIBLE END.

The base has a practical function too. As you lay out your city in a game like *Warcraft* or *Age of Empires*, you are building an interface. Because you built it yourself, you know instantly where to go to initiate an upgrade or spawn a required character.

Some games provide the option of a roving society. Avalon Hill's early strategy game *Incunabula* (itself a PC version of the original *Civilization* boardgame designed by F. G. Tresham) gave players the option to run a Theocracy, Oligarchy, Utopia or Khanate. The last did not build cities, but roamed freely across the map ransacking other civilisations and demanding tribute.

Not having to build a civilisation can be liberating. When you don't have a base of your own to defend, you feel that you have a licence to go pillaging those soft urban characters. But it does deprive the player of the base as a psychological home. Having a base steers your whole perspective on the game. All your transportation radiates out from it, all resources flow back to it. As it grows and thrives, you have a visible marker of your success in the game.

Early RTS games restricted the player to one central base, although in some cases making it possible for you to seize control of enemy bases also. The trend has been towards allowing construction of new bases. It's interesting that

Left: *Electronic Arts'* ***Earth & Beyond****. Placing buildings serves as a mini-game within the bigger picture. Base-building is rarely integrated into the strategic choices of the main game, but still has value as a routine activity that gives the player something to do while mulling over the larger-scale problems.*

Below: ***Silent Storm*** *by Nival Interactive.*

Right: *The ultimate expression of the supremacy of the city: building a Wonder, seen here in Ensemble's* ***Age of Mythology****. This usually entails a massive diversion of resources and is a critical decision by the player. Most often, the Wonder isn't built for its shock-and-awe value, but to turn the endgame into a race. Can other players batter down my walls before the Wonder triggers victory? It would be more interesting if the Wonder didn't finish the game, but instead instituted a specialised bonus for the player's civilisation. Hence a Pharos would improve sight range for all units, Hanging Gardens would improve agricultural yield, and so on.*

HOME 2

many players feel a sentimental attachment to the original base – the old homeworld or birthplace of the player's race – even if later bases are better placed and grow much bigger.

In a strategy game, of course, sentiment is a factor to be exploited like any other. You can divert a player's attention with attacks on his original base while massing to take the base that really matters. Although sometimes that's an erroneous assumption. Burning down the White House doesn't necessarily win you the war.

Sometimes a new base can be built anywhere (e.g. *Warcraft 2*), sometimes only on designated foundation spots around the map (*Age of Mythology*). The argument in favour of the latter approach (apart from making it simpler to represent the map to the opponent AI) is that settlements in real life have a natural spacing that is determined by the flow of resources required to sustain them.

Our view is that this should not be represented by the 'hardwired' solution of fixed foundation points. It would be better to model those resources somehow in the game. Then the player would have an interesting choice – whether to keep his bases widely spaced, or cluster them together. The latter makes them easier to fortify but harder to sustain, and risks the traditional penalty for putting all your eggs in one basket.

That said, it can be annoying in the middle of a fraught real-time war to have to fix buildings that are getting dilapidated, or divert resources to hold a feast day for a bunch of disaffected citizens. That kind of continual maintenance belongs more to turn-based than real-time games. Even there, it calls for careful thought by the designer or else the game simply reduces to a managerial problem in which the player has to guess the optimum set of inputs into an equation posed by the designer. In real life, those decisions can be strategic too. The British government may have decided that the insurgence in Northern Ireland during the 1970s and 1980s was worth the cost as it provided a training ground for urban warfare and policing.
It would be interesting if strategy games could present similar dilemmas.

Savage by S2 Games (right), ***Space Colony*** (left) and ***Stronghold*** from Firefly (above). Placing buildings serves as a mini-game within the bigger picture. Base-building is rarely integrated into the strategic choices of the main game, but still has value as a routine activity that gives the player something to do while mulling over the larger-scale problems.

THE FOG OF WAR

THE ORIGINAL MEANING OF THE FOG OF WAR WAS THE CONFUSION AND UNCERTAINTY THAT INEVITABLY PERVADED ANY ATTEMPT TO UNDERSTAND AND PLAN IN A SITUATION WITH SO MANY COMPLEXITIES. IN STRATEGY GAMES IT HAS COME TO HAVE A MUCH MORE SPECIFIC MEANING. AT THE START OF THE GAME, THE ENTIRE MAP IS OFTEN HIDDEN IN DARKNESS. AS THE PLAYER SCOUTS OUT HIS SURROUNDINGS, THE DARKNESS IS REMOVED.

Below: *This early computer strategy game,* ***Empire: Wargame of the Century*** *by Walter Bright, Mark Baldwin & Northwest Software, shows effective use of fog of war and the extra depth of gameplay from exploration.*

Right: *The* ***Commandos*** *series by Pyro uses very precise fog of war, in that each unit's field of view is calculated. You can see the fields of view being set up in the level editor.*

Left: *Spies should never be overlooked. Information can win a war. In strategy games, spies and scouts can serve many functions – penetrating the fog of war, stealing secrets, finding resources, revealing armies, affecting treaties, causing rebellion, spreading plague and committing arson and sabotage. These units should be versatile and effective, and their value should be reflected in their spawning cost.* ***Civilization*** *by Firaxis has spy units that can reveal enemy information and incite revolt in enemy cities.*

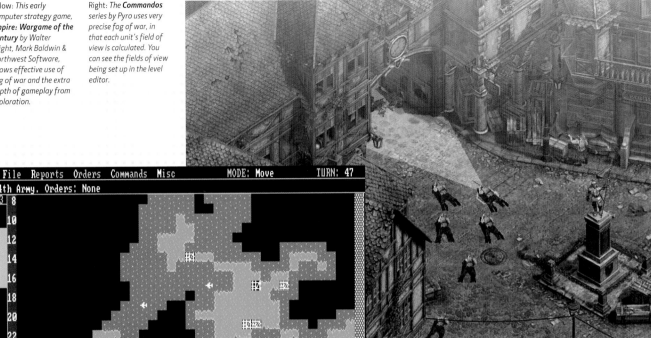

Usually there is a second level to the fog of war. A dimmed area rolls back when the player moves his scouting units on. Hence he has three levels of view: a bright area that shows what his units can currently see, a greyed-out area that shows terrain that has been explored but is not currently in sight range, and the darkness where no scout has yet ventured.

The greyed-out area shows your last intelligence of a region. Early games didn't retain information about enemy buildings in this semi-fog, but latterly it has been common to show buildings as they were when you last saw them. A player in *Age of Kings* can sally over to the enemy huts and stockades he scouted half an hour earlier only to suddenly reveal a magnificent fortress with crenellated walls and stone watchtowers.

As information (and misinformation) play a vital role in strategic planning, the fog of war is ripe for development by the game designer. The ideal is to provide players with a set of features that allow them to deduce the enemy's deployment and progress – and a means of deceiving opponents by clever use of those features.

PENETRATING THE VEIL

In the original design for the game *Warrior Kings*, Dave Morris included a feature whereby armies above a certain size would be visible within the fog of war to opponents, but only the army's battle standard would be seen. You could observe that an enemy army was on the move, but unless you sent scouts to reconnoitre you couldn't be sure how big the army was. It also meant that with careful planning you could secretly bring an army close to a rival city by sending the soldiers in small groups. The battle standard would only appear at the moment those groups combined into an army.

'DEMORALISE THE ENEMY FROM WITHIN BY SURPRISE, TERROR, SABOTAGE AND ASSASSINATION. THIS IS THE WAR OF THE FUTURE.'
ADOLF HITLER

THE FOG OF WAR 2

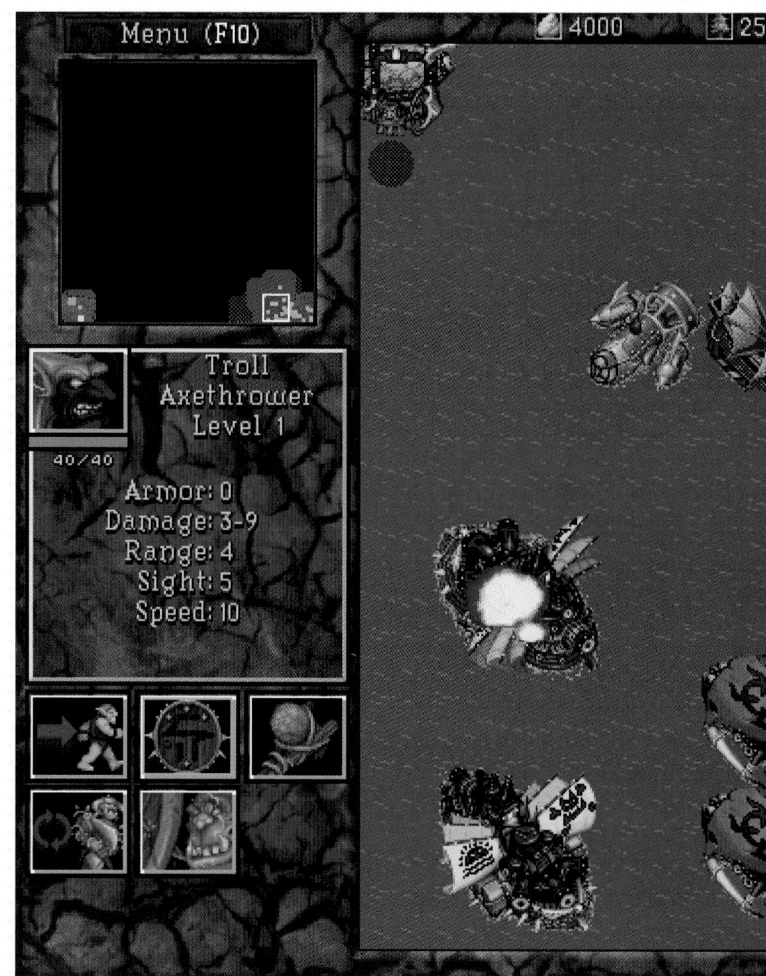

In implementing this feature eventually in the game, Charlie Bewsher at Black Cactus Games had the idea of representing it in a less abstract way. Rather than battle standards, the progress of troops on the march was detectable because it caused birds to fly up in panic out of the trees. Smaller groups of men didn't have this effect, so it became a vivid way of representing the approach of an enemy army – to a player who was vigilant.

That illustrates the evolution of designers' thinking about fog of war. It needs to be more fully integrated into the gameplay – the screeching birds are a great example of how to do it well – but designers have been slow to do so because fog of war is a relatively new feature. In the boardgames where strategy games have their roots, it wasn't really possible to depict unexplored regions. Even in tabletop wargaming moderated by game umpires, fog of war was a cumbersome feature that offered little to gameplay. Computers have revolutionised that. Now exploration and spying are a valid part of strategy gaming.

THE SPIES HAVE IT

'An army without scouts is like a man without eyes or ears', said the T'ang military theorist Chia Lin. Reconnoiting adds an interesting dimension to all strategy games, not only those focused on warfare – but only if the design makes information important.

This may seem an obvious comment, but consider some examples. Broderbund's seminal and brilliant real-time strategy game *The Ancient Art of War* does it right. The only resources are forts, which provide zones of supply for troops and will from time to time spawn new units for the

Right: *Nival Interactive's **Silent Storm**. The rigours of close-up or first – person 3D force a kind of emergent fog of war in that other units aren't visible because you are not looking at them or they are concealed behind objects.*

Far right: *Fog of war is central to Codo International's **Laser Squad: Nemesis**.*

2000

Left: *Blizzard's **Warcraft 2** illustrates many fine design ideas. Scouts are gnomish flying machines and goblin zeppelins – both swift units with no terrain restriction on movement. The very fine and subtle detail is that they have no firepower. This means that the enemy player tends to discount them as a threat. A goblin zeppelin hovering a little way outside your city gates isn't really worth sallying out to shoot down. Or so it seems. If these units had been provided with any kind of weapon, the opponent would not have ignored them. The maps in **Warcraft 2** are dotted with gold mines that never yield quite as much gold as you need. Hence you have to stay mobile, continually setting up new bases as you go, and your scout units are indispensable.*

Above: *In Ensemble's **Age of Mythology**, the highest temple upgrade is Omniscience, which allows you to see everything that your opponents can. This comes – rightly – at a high price, varying with the number of enemy units in the game but rarely less than half the gold you can expect to collect. Once you purchase Ominiscience, you have a lot less gold for building the best units, so not only is the information useful, but buying it is a significant decision that commits you to making it count.*

player controlling them. Forts cannot be destroyed, but they can and do change hands if occupied by another player. You can rarely get enough troops to guard all your forts and still strike out for the flags which are needed for victory. Spies are essential – fast-moving units that give you advance warning of an enemy's approach.

Now consider a game in which you only need a single base that is relatively easy to fortify. Defence is stronger than attack, and resources are so abundant as to be effectively limitless within the duration of the game. It doesn't matter how cleverly the designer has set up features for fog of war, spying and subterfuge – in that game, information is of very little value. The richer and more interesting the strategic domain, the greater the value of spies.

TECHNOLOGY

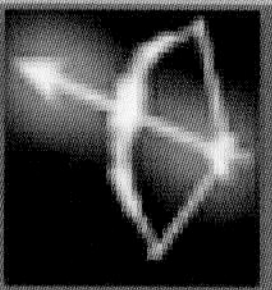

THE TECH TREE IS A FLOW-CHART SHOWING THE DEPENDENCIES OF UPGRADES AND BUILDINGS. IN MOST CASES, OBTAINING AN UPGRADE SUCH AS WHEEL LOCK PISTOLS, FOR EXAMPLE, WILL REQUIRE THE PLAYER FIRST TO HAVE BOUGHT OTHER UPGRADES SUCH AS MACHINE TOOLING, WHICH IN TURN MIGHT REQUIRE THE METALWORKING UPGRADE PLUS THE FURNACE BUILDING, AND SO ON.

WHAT IS THE POINT OF A TECH TREE?

The tech tree forms a game within a game and encourages you to plan for the big picture. Other than providing the player with small rewards to track his progress, it gives structure to the 'story' of each level. Regardless of the actions of other players, you can perceive a beginning, middle and end as you progress from bearskin-clad caveman to citizen hoplite to professional soldier – or whatever life-path the theme of the game dictates.

The tech tree catalyses potential opportunities to win ('inciting incidents' in story terms) because the player further along the tech tree has an incentive to hit other players hard right after a significant upgrade. However, it has to be said that in most games you don't get to see other players' positions on the tech tree, so the incentive is lost.

Left: ***Age of Mythology*** *from Ensemble Studios.*

Above left: ***Command & Conquer: Generals*** *from Electronic Arts.*

Right: ***Alien Nations*** *by Jowood.*

Below: *Concept art for* ***Haegemonia*** *by Digital Reality.*

Upgrades on the tech tree are paid for with resources and, as well as enabling further upgrades, may have one or more of the following effects:

- Increased range, speed, etc., for units and buildings
- Ability to spawn new units
- Ability to create new buildings
- Special player abilities (reveal map, etc.)

In most strategy games, decisions on the tech tree are trivial. There is a given optimum order to carrying out those upgrades, at least in the early stages. The basic purpose of the tech tree is therefore not to provide another layer of choice to deepen gameplay, but simply to give the new player a quick reward. It is easy to learn the optimum path up the tech tree, and it gives players a comforting routine to ease them into a game.

Technology creates strange bedfellows. For instance, the different resource requirements and abilities of races such as *Starcraft*'s Protoss and Zerg tends to make them natural allies – even against other Protoss and Zerg players.

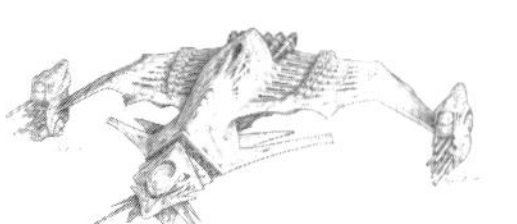   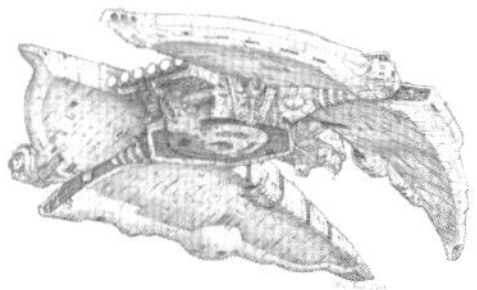 

TECHNOLOGY 2

FROM FLINT KNIVES TO PHASERS

Perhaps there is something in the strategy genre that fosters grandiosity. Or perhaps it is only that pondering strategic choices leads one inevitably to a millennial perspective. Whatever the reason, many games from *Civilization* to *Empire Earth* seek to simulate the whole story of human progress – sometimes in one afternoon or less.

In those games, whole groups of upgrades are made available by progressing between eras – from the Neolithic to the Bronze Age, and so on. The eras themselves are upgrades that act as filters, opening up new layers in the tree. Era upgrades are rarely time-dependent, other than indirectly because of the need to collect enough resources and buildings to activate the upgrade. The famous 'Bronze

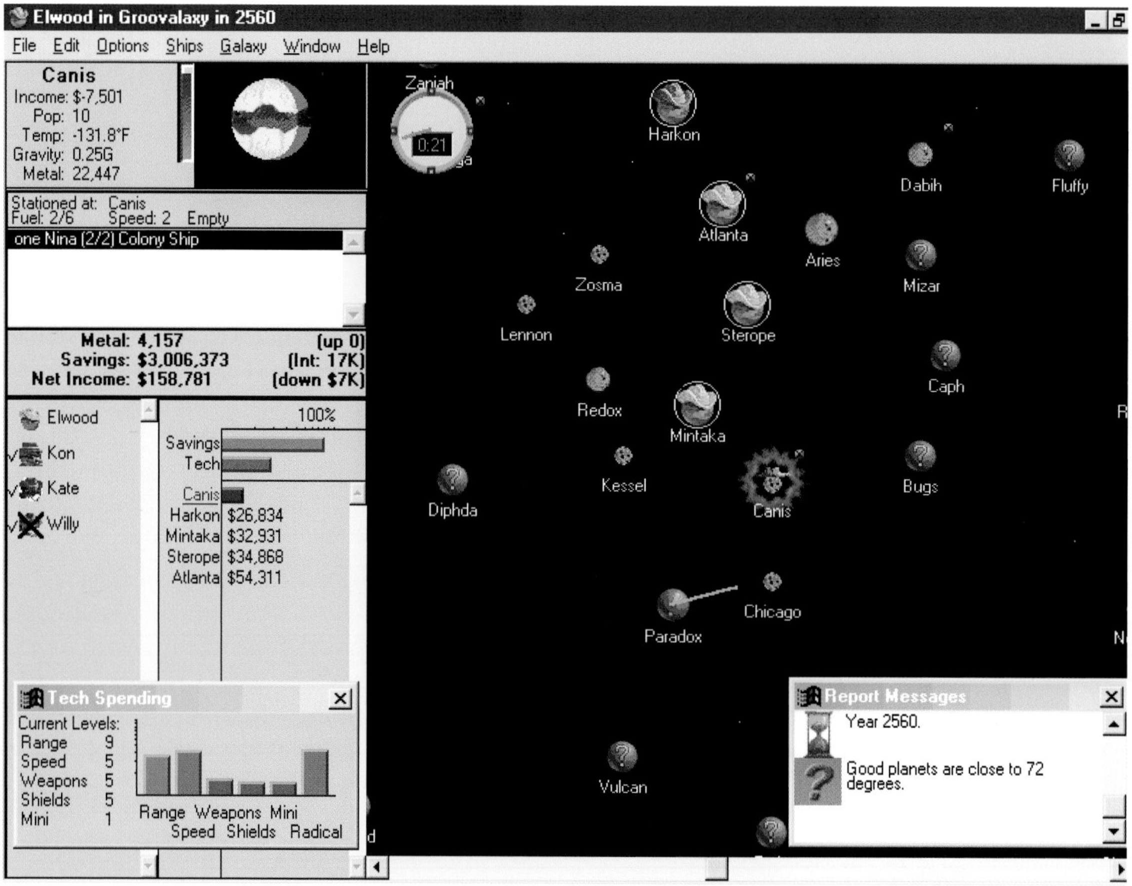

*In New World Computing's **Spaceward Ho**, an early game of interstellar colonisation, players had to allocate resources at each colony between defence, terraforming and research. Pumping more money into research didn't necessarily guarantee new technology, and discovery took time, making this a nail-bitingly tense classic of the genre.*

Age Rush' of *Age of Empires* took around nine minutes, for example, if you completed all tasks in the right order.

Some games link the tech tree to the collection of items, such as relics or crates. It is also possible to close off parts of the tech tree that the player can only unlock by achieving objectives such as exploration or finding a specific character. These elements provide designers with a way to steer progress in a campaign game.

Sometimes research on the tech tree only takes place between levels. In *XCOM: Enemy Unknown*, for instance, you didn't buy upgrades during a mission, you acquired them in downtime between levels.

BUT IS IT PROGRESS?

Progress up the tech tree shouldn't just become a rush to get every upgrade. It ought to involve choices. You can have this or that, but not both. Broad choices that affect the focus of a civilisation – whether it puts its emphasis on economy or defence or missiles, and so on – are interesting and reflect the way the world is. Optimising every attribute is not only unrealistic, it's boring.

When you can get all the upgrades, it's not as interesting as having limited resources, etc., and having to pick the upgrades that suit your strategy. The ideal would be allowing players to switch from some upgrades to others but maybe not having all at once.

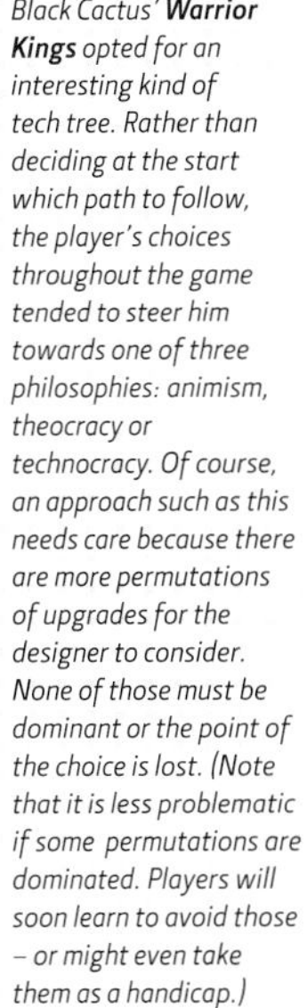

*Black Cactus' **Warrior Kings** opted for an interesting kind of tech tree. Rather than deciding at the start which path to follow, the player's choices throughout the game tended to steer him towards one of three philosophies: animism, theocracy or technocracy. Of course, an approach such as this needs care because there are more permutations of upgrades for the designer to consider. None of those must be dominant or the point of the choice is lost. (Note that it is less problematic if some permutations are dominated. Players will soon learn to avoid those – or might even take them as a handicap.)*

UPGRADES CAN BE MADE GLOBALLY TO ALL EXISTING UNITS, OR THEY CAN ENABLE YOU TO CREATE A NEW IMPROVED UNIT BUT YOUR EXISTING ONES STAY UNCHANGED, OR THEY CAN ENABLE YOU TO PAY TO IMPROVE EACH EXISTING UNIT.

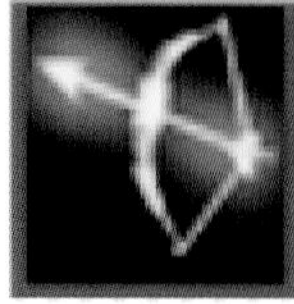

WHEN TO GO GLOBAL

Mindscape's game *War Wind* did it the third way. You put units in a training hall to equip them with the upgrade. It didn't work out very well because there was only one door, so when you put a couple of units into the hall, the first one in would get its upgrade and then you'd need to get the other one to move to let him out. Even with a door on each side (the training hall as conveyor belt) it would still have meant a lot of micro-management in calling your units back to base for upgrading.

Having upgrades that apply instantly and globally will encourage players to use aggressive strategies. Here's why. If suddenly all my marines get a 20 per cent increase in firepower, and if I'm ahead of the other player, I'm going to want to use my newly acquired lead before he catches up.

If, on the other hand, the upgrade simply allows me to build a new super-marine unit but leaves my existing marines unmodified, it confers no immediate advantage. It could in fact even be a disadvantage. Say I had to pay 2000 dilithium credits for that upgrade, while my opponent spent the same money on a few dozen new (non-upgraded) marines instead. At just about the time I'm starting to train my first super-marine, those 24 ordinary marines show up at my base and turn it into rubble.

Potentially that's one of the interesting choices that define pure gameplay. However, there are other ways of implementing a tech tree. For example, in *XCOM: Enemy Unknown*, the player has to capture alien artefacts and wait while his scientists analyse the technology in order to

The ends justify the means!
***Civilization 3** by Firaxis.*

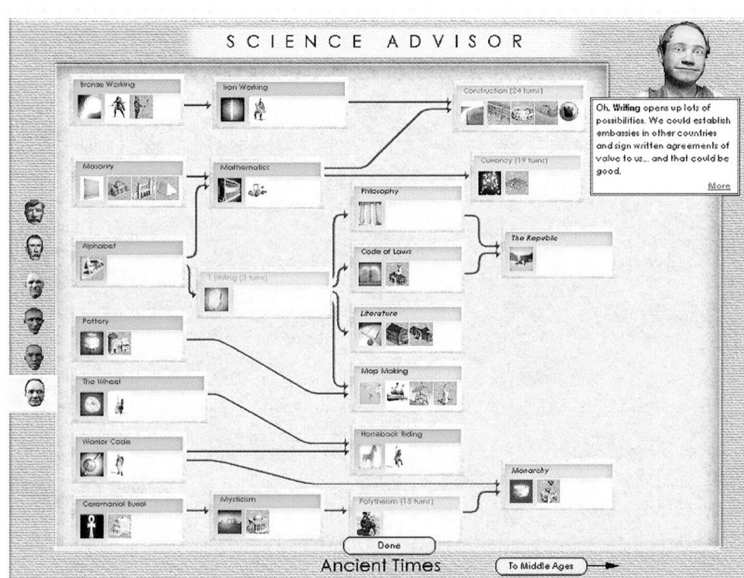

duplicate it. Another method, used originally in Avalon Hill's *Incunabula*, requires the player to trade in order to acquire enhancements such as metalworking, literacy and medicine.

The problem of having tech tree progress run off exactly the same resources as the central gameplay mechanisms (usually conquest) is that it leads to difficult decisions, but not necessarily interesting ones. Paying that dilithium to upgrade the marines isn't a strategic conundrum so much as a pure gamble. If, on the other hand, the technology the player needs grows out of an activity that is in tension with some other objective – for instance, it depends on trade in a game that is mostly about warfare – then you start to get an interesting game.

A COMMON ELEMENT IN MANY RTS GAMES WITH 'HARD' TECH TREES IS TO DISALLOW THE USE OF UNITS OR UPGRADES THAT WERE AVAILABLE IN EARLIER LEVELS. THE PURPOSE OF DOING THIS IS TO STEER THE GAME EXPERIENCE.

BACK TO SQUARE ONE

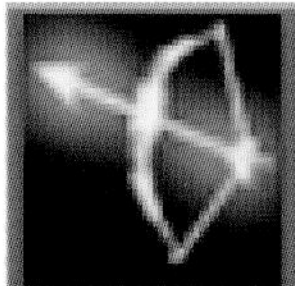

Making yourself king of the hill in CDV Software's ***Codename: Panzers.***

The designer is saying, OK, you know you could easily handle an assault on the ice mine if you had retro-grav bombs, but now you're going to have to find a different solution because retro-grav isn't available in this level.

The trouble is that no matter how ingenious the story excuse (retro-grav causing a destabilisation of the planet's crust or whatever) it's absolutely obvious that it's just the designer forcing you to play it his way. And here's the thing: that kind of design is really, really irritating. Games are all about putting the player in control of the entertainment experience. Using a clunky story device to justify hobbling the player's choices is big but it's not clever.

Below: *Or mastering an entire continent in* ***Crusader Kings*** *by Paradox.*

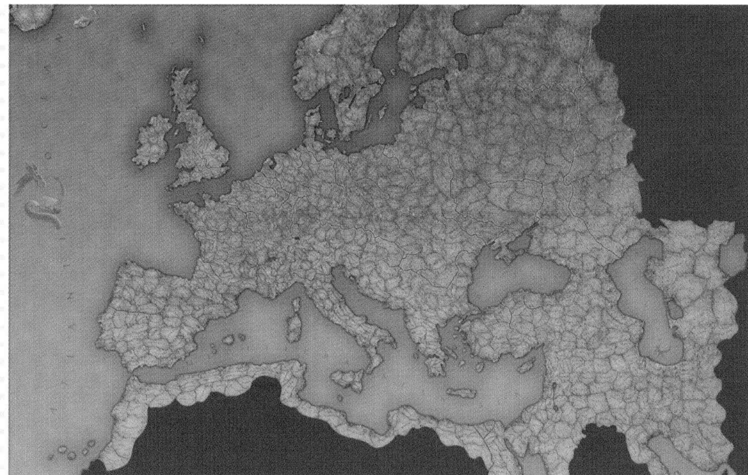

Right: *Or just fighting the axis of evil in* ***Commandos 3*** *from Pyro Studios.*

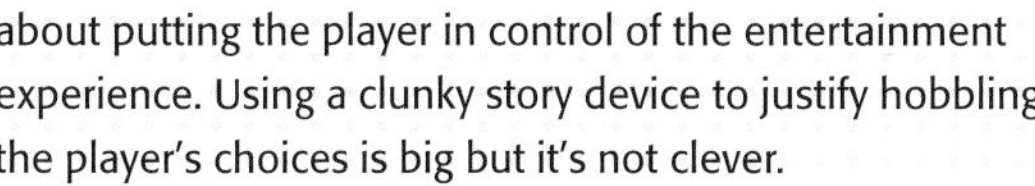

There are other ways to do it without the designer getting all authorial. One is to have retro-grav really destabilise ice crusts. If the player's base breaks off and goes flying into space, then he's only got himself to blame.

Alternatively, make the retro-grav technology available but restrict the supporting costs. If you need heavy metals to build retro-grav bombs – well, this is a frozen ice-planet after all. You're not saying the player can't build those bombs; you're just not giving him the materials to do it with.

SUPPLY

Below: ***Perimeter*** *by KD Labs.*

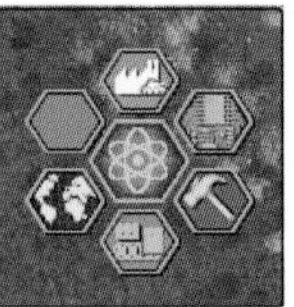

THE EARLY RTS GAMES ALL FEATURED SUPPLY LINES IN ONE FORM OR ANOTHER. ***DUNE 2****, THE DADDY OF THEM ALL, REPRESENTED SUPPLY BY REQUIRING THE PLAYER TO BUILD A NETWORK OF ROADS. YOU COULD ONLY PLACE BUILDINGS ADJACENT TO ROADS, SO THIS SET A LIMIT ON THE RATE THAT CITIES COULD EXPAND AND PROVIDED AN IMMEDIATE CYCLE OF PROBLEM AND REWARD.*

You could see that you needed to extend your road across the bridge before you could place a bunch of defensive turrets, so you'd rush in with some tanks, take the bridgehead, and rapidly build the road across to secure your new front.

Both *Command & Conquer* and the original *Warcraft* followed suit, but later games have tended to abandon this feature even though it gave at least a partial sense of supply lines. It didn't affect units, only buildings – in effect being a 'power grid' into which buildings had to hook up in order to access resources. But it had the virtue of simplicity so it's not immediately obvious why the current generation of RTS games have dropped it.

Looking back to the grandfather of RTS, *The Ancient Art of War*, we can see how supply can be problematic. There, players were just told whether their units were in or out of supply – a function that varied inversely with the distance from friendly occupied forts. Units out of supply became fatigued and would move more slowly and fight less effectively until they came back in range. This worked fine in *Ancient Art of War* because it was a single-player game and it had a fairly sedate pace at the strategic level. In a modern, multiplayer, fast-moving RTS there's no room for factors that the player can't see at a glance.

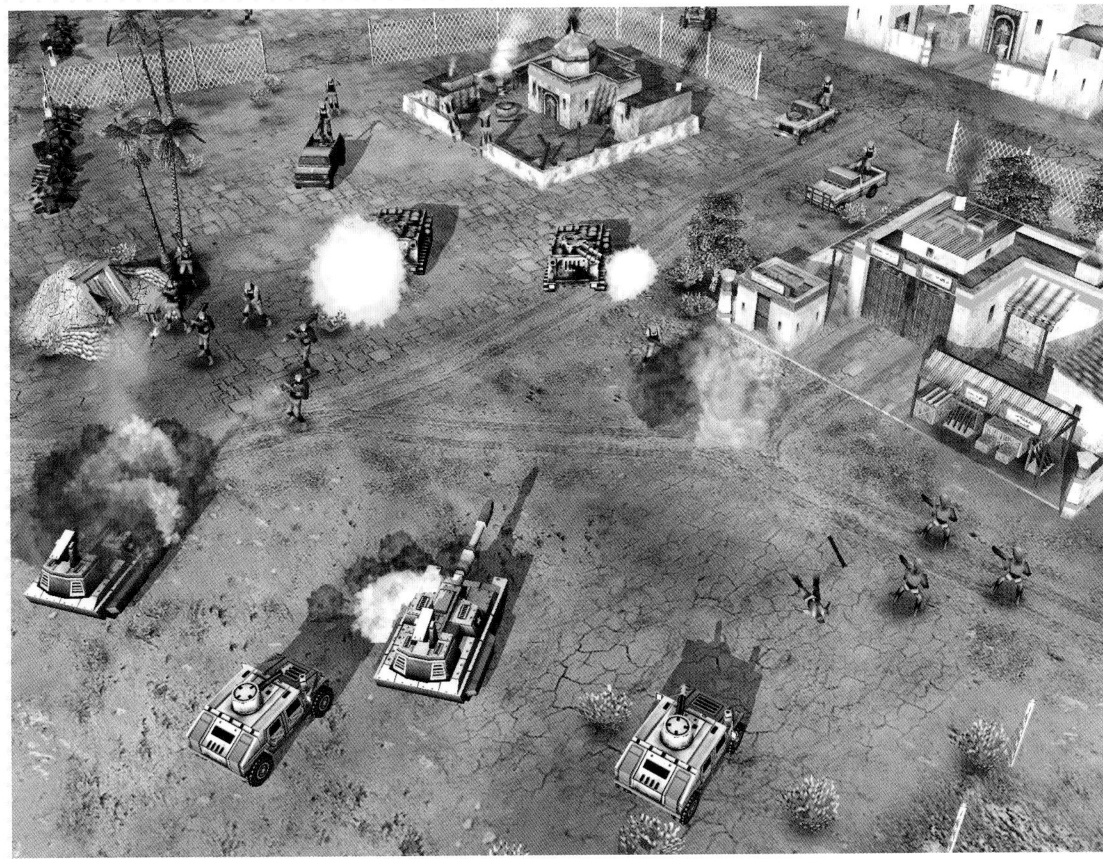

Left: ***Command & Conquer: Generals*** *from EA Pacific/ Westwood Studios.*

SUPPLY 2

IGNACIO PÉREZ of Pyro Studios warns: 'It's difficult to make supply lines work in a real-time game. They're more a turn-based feature and not always well received by the type of gamer who is looking for a less cerebral experience. Even most board games of the war-simulation variety have the option of playing without supply lines. So if this is a feature not very much welcomed by turn-based gamers, imagine the reaction of real-time gamers. I have played a lot of board games myself and I was never a big fan of supply lines. Although they add realism, most of the time they are just tedious to use.'

INVASION OR INFECTION?

But consider the baby as well as the bathwater. In a game like *Age of Kings*, the absence of supply lines means that you can send a single peasant into enemy territory and there's nothing to stop him building a whole fortified city and pumping out an army of infantry, cavalry and artillery. That feels wrong and it makes it hard for a new player to tackle game situations based on prior experience. The new player might reasonably suppose that allowing a solitary enemy peasant to slip past his sentry patrols isn't going to matter much.

THE CARROT NOT THE STICK

It's worth having some kind of supply-line feature in any RTS because without it you get a pretty strange kind of warfare. The drawback is when the supply feature becomes complicated, or hard to see, or is set up in such a way as to penalise the player.

Consider a game in which unsupplied troops get weaker or run out of ammunition. That's bad design. The player should be rewarded for doing things right, not punished for doing it wrong. So a better way to handle supply – if you're going to have it at all – would be as in Black Cactus's *Warrior Kings*, where injured troops with a line of supply back to their city will recover hit points over time.

1503 AD: The New World
from Sunflowers.

Left: *CDV Software's* ***Codename: Panzers***.

Left: ***Civilization 3*** *employs a simplified supply system that still allows for rewarding gameplay. Cities must be connected by a road network to access resources. This allows an attacking player to detach a city from its network by destroying the surrounding roads, thus softening the city up for attack. After capturing it, he can then rebuild the roads to join up with his own resource network.*

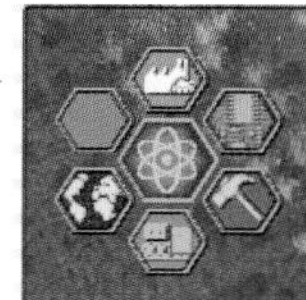

SUPPLY 3

Below: ***Massive Assault*** *from Wargaming.net.*

Left: ***Silent Storm*** *by Nival – unusual for a strategy game in that it takes the player right into the 3D world rather than watching from above.*

Left: ***Haegemonia*** *by Digital Reality.*

Right: *Eidos's* ***Warzone 2100****, developed by Pumpkin Studios, presented players with an interesting supply trade-off on the campaign level. Buildings for unit production could either be built on the current level, in which case they provided units quickly; or they could be placed off-map back at the player's home base, in which case it took time for new units to arrive but with the advantage that an off-map building can provide units in later levels, too.*

Such a system leads naturally to the inclusion of troop experience levels, because now it becomes worth rotating your units and allowing them time to heal up. You end up with seasoned veterans. And then you have the interesting choice of when to commit those veterans. Sometimes you have to risk your crack troops in order to strike a decisive blow.

The designer still has to decide how to depict supply on screen. *Warrior Kings* featured quartermaster wagons that would trundle from the player's home castle carrying the resources needed to resupply troops in the field. The player didn't need to keep telling the wagons where to go; he just assigned them to an army and the AI did the rest. The feature allowed players to disrupt each other's supply lines by intercepting and looting the wagons. You also had the option of launching an attack without wagons, but it was a risk.

BREAD OR PAIN?

In conclusion – are supply lines worth the hassle? ***FREDRIK LINDGREN*** of Paradox Entertainment: 'Of course it depends on what kind of game you want to create. But supply lines can be interesting and challenging, as well as demanding higher levels of strategic thinking than just a battle on its own.'

There are good and bad ways to handle supply in any strategy game. Real-time obliges the designer to streamline any supply rules, but it is worth thinking about ways to do that because the inclusion of supply can lead to a richer game. Above all, any solution the designer implements needs to avoid bogging the players down in micro-management. The player's opponent must always be other players, not the game design itself.

Jowood's ***Spellforce***

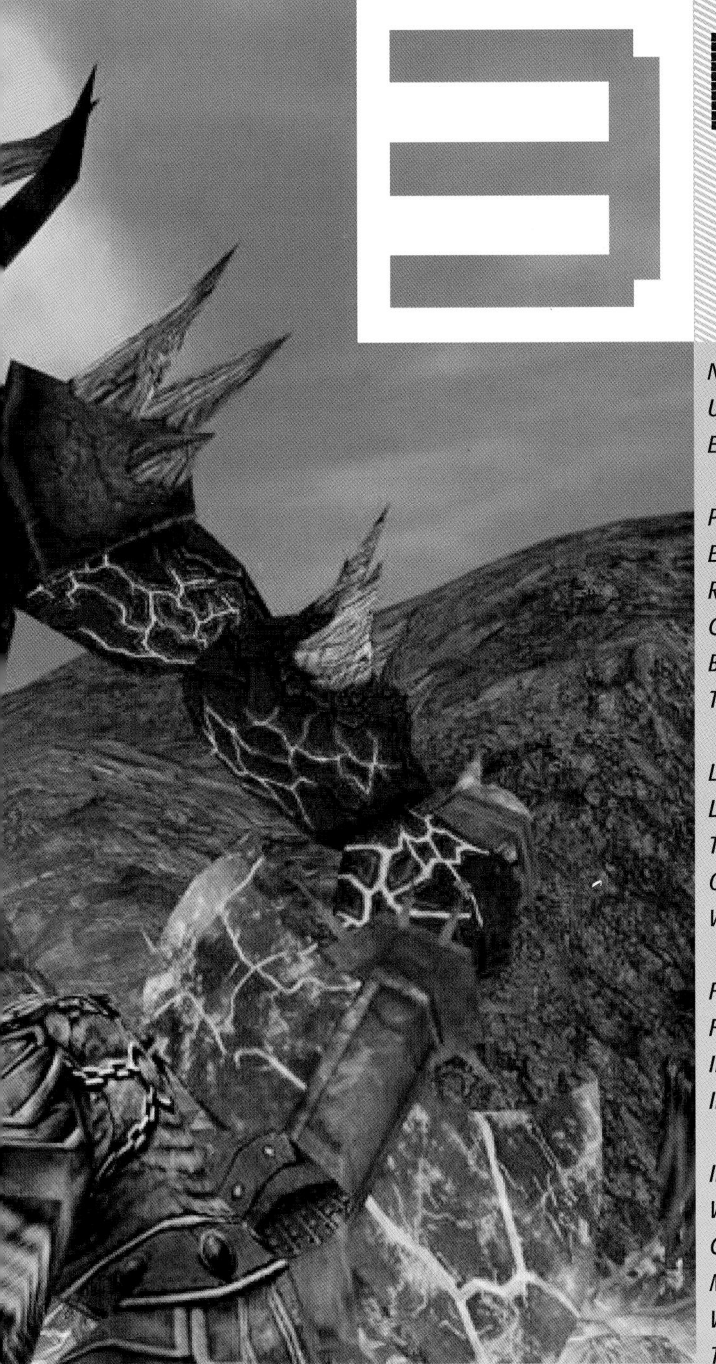

SECTION

3 DESIGN

NOW THAT WE'VE TAKEN A LOOK AT WHAT IT IS THAT DEFINES AND UNDERLIES THE STRATEGY GENRE, THIS THIRD SECTION OF THE BOOK EXAMINES THE WAY THAT THOSE ELEMENTS ARE ASSEMBLED INTO A GAME.

*AN EXAMPLE FROM **WARRIOR KINGS** WILL SHOW HOW THE PROCESS OF DESIGN INVOLVES CREATING A SHORTHAND VERSION OF THE ENVIRONMENT THE GAME IS MODELLING SO THAT PLAYERS GET THE RESULTS THEY INTUITIVELY EXPECT. IN THE EARLY DESIGN STAGE OF THE GAME, THE GOAL WAS TO RECREATE AUTHENTIC-SEEMING MEDIEVAL BATTLES. ONE OF THE FEATURES THAT THE CLIENT (EIDOS) WANTED WAS TO HAVE FORMATIONS THAT ACTUALLY HAD A PURPOSE IN THE GAME.*

MEDIEVAL SOLDIERS DIDN'T USE FORMATIONS JUST BECAUSE THEY LOOKED PRETTY. TROOPS IN COLUMN FORMATION TRAVEL QUICKLY, BUT LINE FORMATION IS BETTER WHEN THE FIGHTING STARTS. A LINE IS ROBUST; THE TROOPS BEHIND GIVE PHYSICAL WEIGHT AND MORAL SUPPORT. ON THE OTHER HAND, IT'S SLOW AND IT'S VULNERABLE TO OUTFLANKING. THAT'S WHEN YOU NEED A SQUARE FORMATION, AND SO ON.

THE GAME'S DESIGNER (DAVE MORRIS) USED TROOP FORMATION TO DEPICT THEIR STANDING ORDERS. TROOPS IN SCATTERED FORMATION WILL SKIRMISH, SNIPING AT THE ENEMY BUT RETREATING IF THREATENED; TROOPS IN LINE WILL TRUDGE DOGGEDLY FORWARDS INTO BATTLE; AND SO ON.

*MORALE IS IRRITATING IN AN RTS BECAUSE ITS EFFECTS ARE INVISIBLE TO THE PLAYER. ALL THE SAME, THERE NEEDED TO BE SOME WAY IN **WARRIOR KINGS** TO REFLECT THE EXTRA ROBUSTNESS THAT COMES FROM FIGHTING IN A WELL-DRILLED FORMATION. A GROUP OF MEN FIGHTING IN LINE IS TOUGHER THAN THE SUM OF ITS PARTS. THE WAY THE FIRST-PASS DESIGN IMPLEMENTED THIS WAS TO HAVE UNITS ON THE KILLING FRONT SHARING DAMAGE WITH THE REST OF THE UNIT.*

INTERFACE

INTERFACE IS THE LAYER THROUGH WHICH THE PLAYER ANALYSES AND INTERACTS WITH THE GAME WORLD. IN GENERAL, THE MOVE IS TOWARDS MAKING THIS 'PRESENTATION AND PARTICIPATION LAYER' AS TRANSPARENT AS POSSIBLE. THE TREND IN ACTION-ADVENTURE, FOR EXAMPLE, HAS RECENTLY BEEN TO DISPENSE WITH HEALTH BARS AND AMMO COUNT.

Information like that can be directly depicted in the game environment: a wounded character limps and bleeds, you can break open a revolver and look at the chambers. So designers are happily doing away with many of the old conventions of an abstract interface.

In strategy and management games, that's not so easy. The player needs to get a lot of data from many sources in the game, and also to interact on multiple levels from tycoon or tyrant down to the lowliest worker. Dumping tasks onto the AI is only valid if those tasks are routine. Where there is any element of strategy, the player will want to be able to interact. Wars can be lost because tiberium harvesters take the wrong route home.

Bullfrog's *Dungeon Keeper* sports a superb interface that makes it possible to keep track of all the player's monsters, see what they are doing, and select them quickly when they're needed. The game is complex but the interface makes it seem simple. You can grab monsters straight off the interface tables and drop them back into the world. Fine control is not easy once monsters start fighting – as more pile in, you soon get the 'pudding of monsters' effect shown here. But this is less important, since *Dungeon Keeper* is primarily a management game with only a high-level strategy layer.

'First, the designer has to create a system that the player can buy into, where the diverse elements seem believable, then create basic strategies using the game mechanics (maps, units, skills), and finally create ways to counter all the previous strategies. Keep in mind that this is more a matter of player perception and expectations than life-like attributes and strategies.'

DANNY BELANGER, *Director of Internal Development at Strategy First*

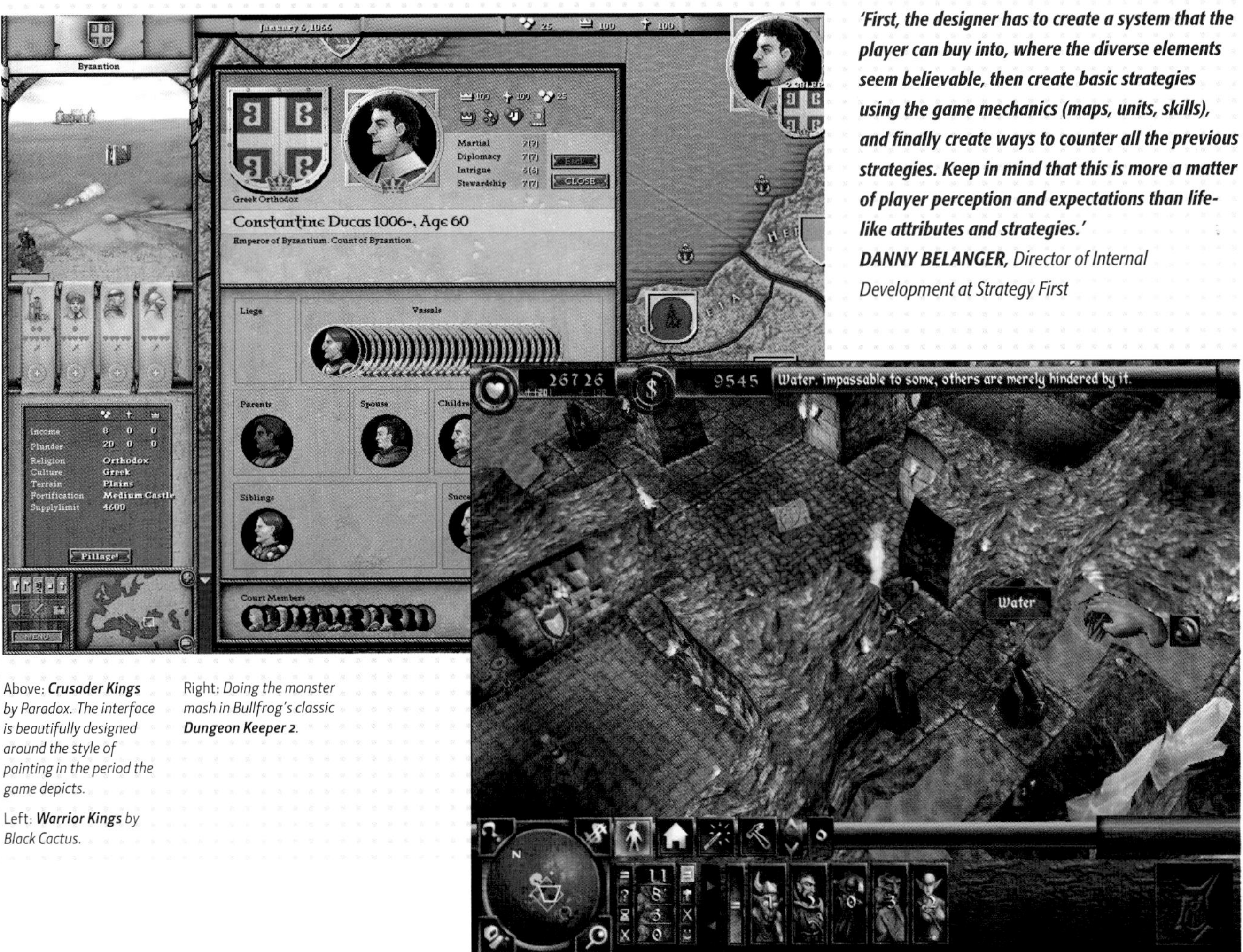

Above: ***Crusader Kings*** *by Paradox. The interface is beautifully designed around the style of painting in the period the game depicts.*

Left: ***Warrior Kings*** *by Black Cactus.*

Right: *Doing the monster mash in Bullfrog's classic* ***Dungeon Keeper 2****.*

Left: *Drag units straight from the bar in* ***Dungeon Keeper 2.***

INTERFACE 2

A classic pattern has evolved for strategy game interfaces. It's interesting to note how the pattern has changed over time. *Command & Conquer* and *Warcraft* both ran the control interface down the side of the screen. The window showing the action in those games looks cramped by today's standards. With the move to isometric and then full 3D, the view is logically now rectangular rather than square, as in the old top-down 2D days. Now the windows showing the selected unit data, available actions and so on customarily run along the bottom of the screen.

3D has brought its own problems. How much control should the player have over the camera? The answer is, not much. There are plenty of other big decisions to make in a strategy game (especially an RTS game) without having to keep repositioning the camera. Of course, the fact that it's possible to make that statement so emphatically shows that most modern strategy games are only using 3D as eye candy. In many cases, as far as the gameplay is concerned, they might as well be in top-down 2D. The few that fully make use of the 3D environment – such as *Populous 3* and *Black & White* – are still exceptions.

A litmus test: if the interface looks cluttered, it could be that the design is, too. If you're designing a strategy game, look to see where you could embed parts of the interface within the world. For example, attaching commands to buildings allows players to build the interface as they go and avoids drill-down menus in which a player can get lost.

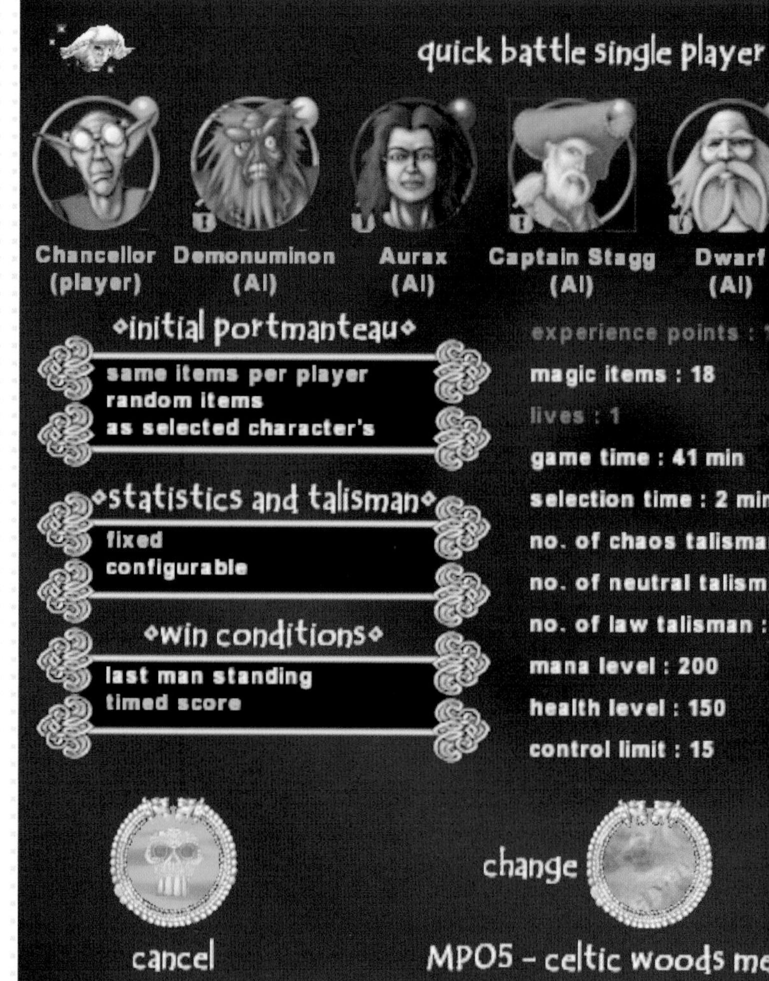

Below: *Climax's* ***Art of Magic*** *lets players choose the size and difficulty of the game level. The in-game interface has pleasingly solid icons that look as though you should be able to pick them out of the screen.*

Left: *Less is more. Blizzard's original* ***Warcraft*** *featured just a handful of units but had extraordinary depth of gameplay.*

'Better graphics and physics may be exploited more in future, but I don't think it will have any radical impact on gameplay. My main argument for this is that currently we can convey just about any gameplay mechanism if we so desire. Yes, better technology might be able to make something like fog of war look cooler, but the gameplay underneath will still remain the same. Moving forward there is a danger that designers and coders will get carried away with the opportunities for creating more complex systems. In doing so they lose sight of the reason why they are doing it. If implementing a rule that pistoleers can't fire their weapons in the rain were to result in the creation of a whole dynamic system, then the game is likely to suffer from over-design.'
PAUL TWYNHOLM*, Designer of* ***Art of Magic***

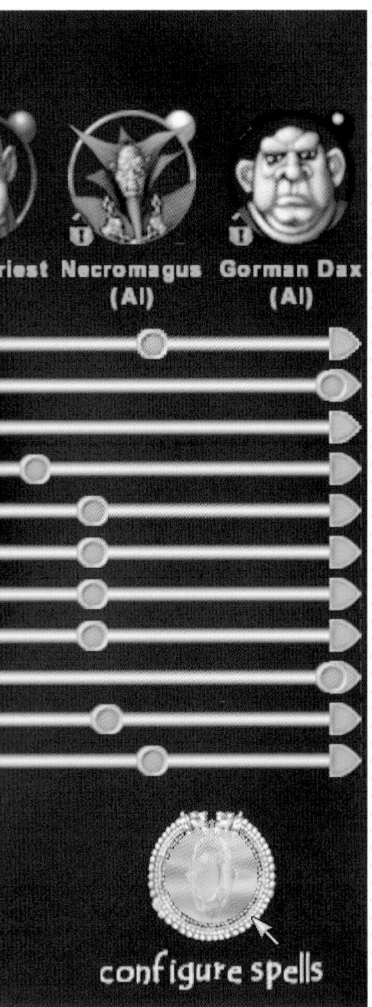

Step back from the design and ask: what are the first decisions the player will be making in the game? What can I do with the interface to help the player?

Buckminster Fuller said: 'I never think about beauty, I only think about how to solve a problem. But when I have finished, if the solution isn't beautiful then I know it's wrong.'

The interface is the dashboard. If it isn't elegant, if people can't make it work for them rather than the other way around – then no matter how powerful the engine under the bonnet, everything else has gone to waste.

Right: ***War Times*** *from IS Games*

'ONLY CONNECT,' ADVISED E. M. FORSTER, CITING THE ONE INVIOLABLE RULE OF ENTERTAINMENT. IF THE GAME – OR NOVEL, OR FILM – FAILS TO ENGAGE, THEN WE AREN'T GOING TO CARE. IF WE DON'T CARE, WE'RE GOING TO FIND A BETTER WAY TO SPEND OUR LEISURE TIME. ***QUOD ERAT DEMONSTRANDUM.***

WHO NEEDS A HERO?

RTS designers are chasing Forster's dictum because the experience of directing a battle from 1000 feet up has plenty of potential for cerebral excitement, but it can be hard to care.

Ever since *Starcraft*, heroes are back in fashion. Used properly, heroes give us a direct link to the events of a battle. Stories involving the deaths of thousands are abstract. It becomes real and immediate when you can personalise the action. That's why Homer describes the events of *The Iliad* as though the fighting were being carried out by a handful of superhuman heroes, even though it's clear that his ur-text involves whole armies. When Achilles sallies forth he has the Myrmidons at his side, even though the poem makes it sound as though he's a Marvel Comics hero standing alone against the foe.

Very often, the hero in an RTS is just a device to let the designer flex his or her authorial muscles. You can see this particularly when the mission objectives require you to keep the hero alive or you can't finish the level. If the hero gets killed and you have to revert to a saved game to get him back, that rather defeats the object of having a hero in the first place. You're supposed to believe in the game world more because of this character. Having to molly-coddle him through a level achieves the opposite effect. Eventually, if you don't want to reload a previous save every time he gets killed, you're going to keep him well back out of the action and just try to get through the level without him. And then he's no hero, he's just a thorn in your side.

Sometimes a level requires you to get the hero to a certain point to unlock the vault, repair the ship, activate the time bomb. But then he's nothing but a puppet for the authorial aims of the designer. You can't feel any kind of emotional attachment to a key.

Jowood's ***Spellforce*** *mixes a role-playing game with strategy making your character the hero.*

This concept drawing is from Blizzard's ***Warcraft 3****.*

WHO NEEDS A HERO? 2

THE THIN RED LINE

If a game is going to include a hero character, he can't be a souped-up version of a standard unit. You won't convince me that this is El Cid when I can plainly see he's just a cavalryman with +300 hit points. He has to have special abilities that make him different from any other game character, if only so that there are interesting choices about when and how to use him.

During battles in the Crusades, a herald used to be assigned to hold the reins of the Templar Grandmaster's horse. All the Templar cavalry would sit there champing at the bit. On a signal from the Frankish commander, the herald would hand the Grandmaster his reins and get out of the way fast. It was the medieval equivalent of lighting the blue touch-paper and retiring to a safe distance.

This provides us with one way of using heroes in games. If they are at least partly autonomous, they become characters we can believe in. You still have gameplay choices – whether to bring them to the battle, where to position them, and when and if to let them off the leash. What happens then may be surprising. It may force you to rethink your strategy. But crucially it's you, the player, who will be creating this story.

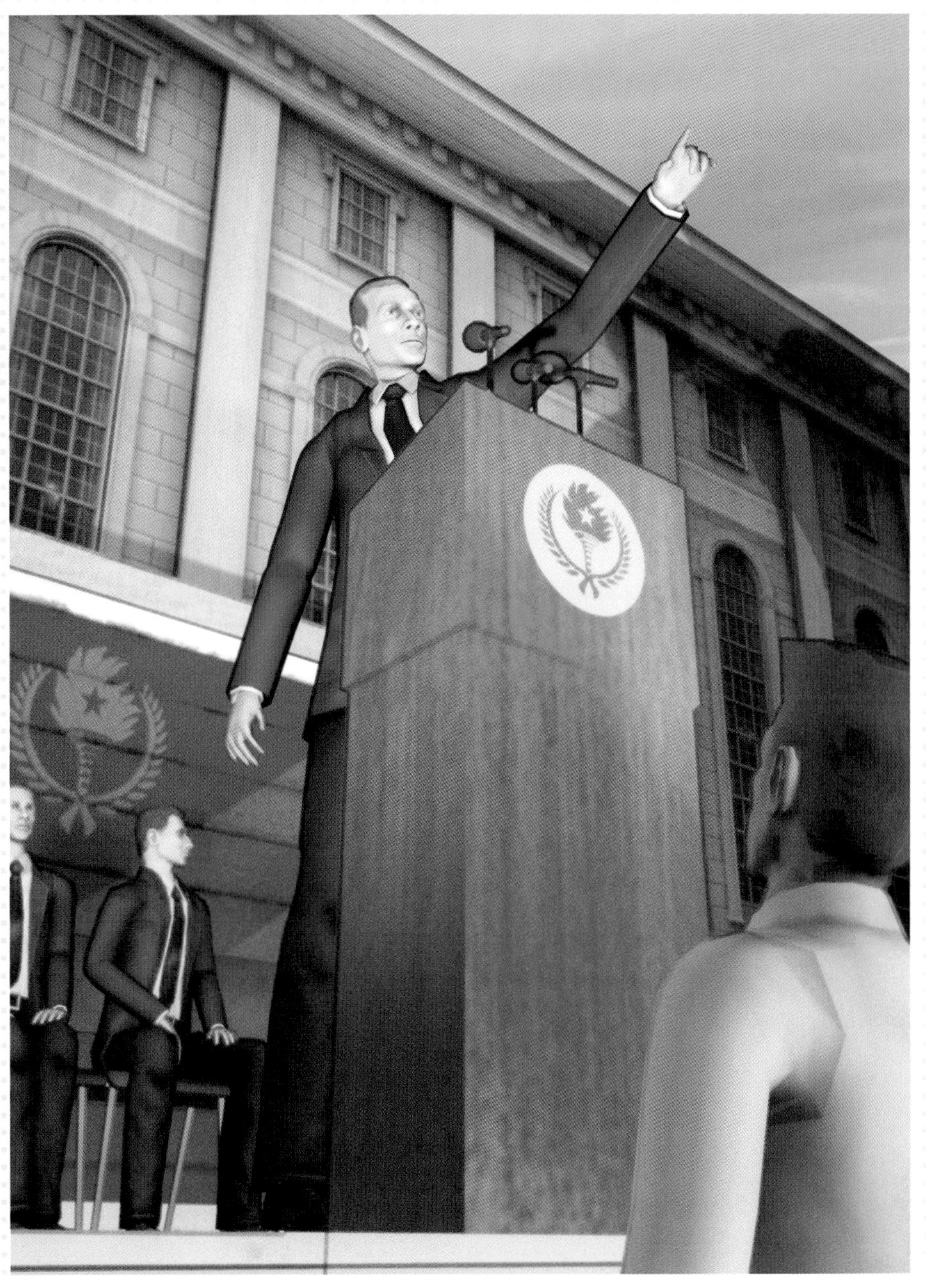

*'Where laws end, tyranny begins.' A dialectical hero from **Republic: The Revolution** by Elixir Studios.*

CHAIN OF COMMAND

Another quite different way to use heroes is the chain-of-command method. Here the player issues orders to the hero and those orders are conveyed down through the hierarchy. So you might tell Alexander the Great to attack an enemy detachment, then select one of his Companions to give a more specific order – say a flanking attack on another group supporting the main enemy – which will cause that Companion and his personal complement of foot soldiers to peel off from the main attack.

That's using the heroes as an 'officer interface', which is valid from a game-control perspective since it saves having to deal with dozens or hundreds of troops at one time. Returning to the theme of emotional connection, however, it's a step in the opposite direction. It appeals to the chess player, not the gamer who wants to experience thrills and hope and loss.

Is the only answer to strike some compromise in the tension between the two? Filmmakers in Europe have long believed that films can be commercial or they can be artistic. Hollywood has shown us time and again that they can be both. Thesis and antithesis can lead to synthesis. Perhaps what we need in RTS today is a new breed of dialectical hero.

BALANCE

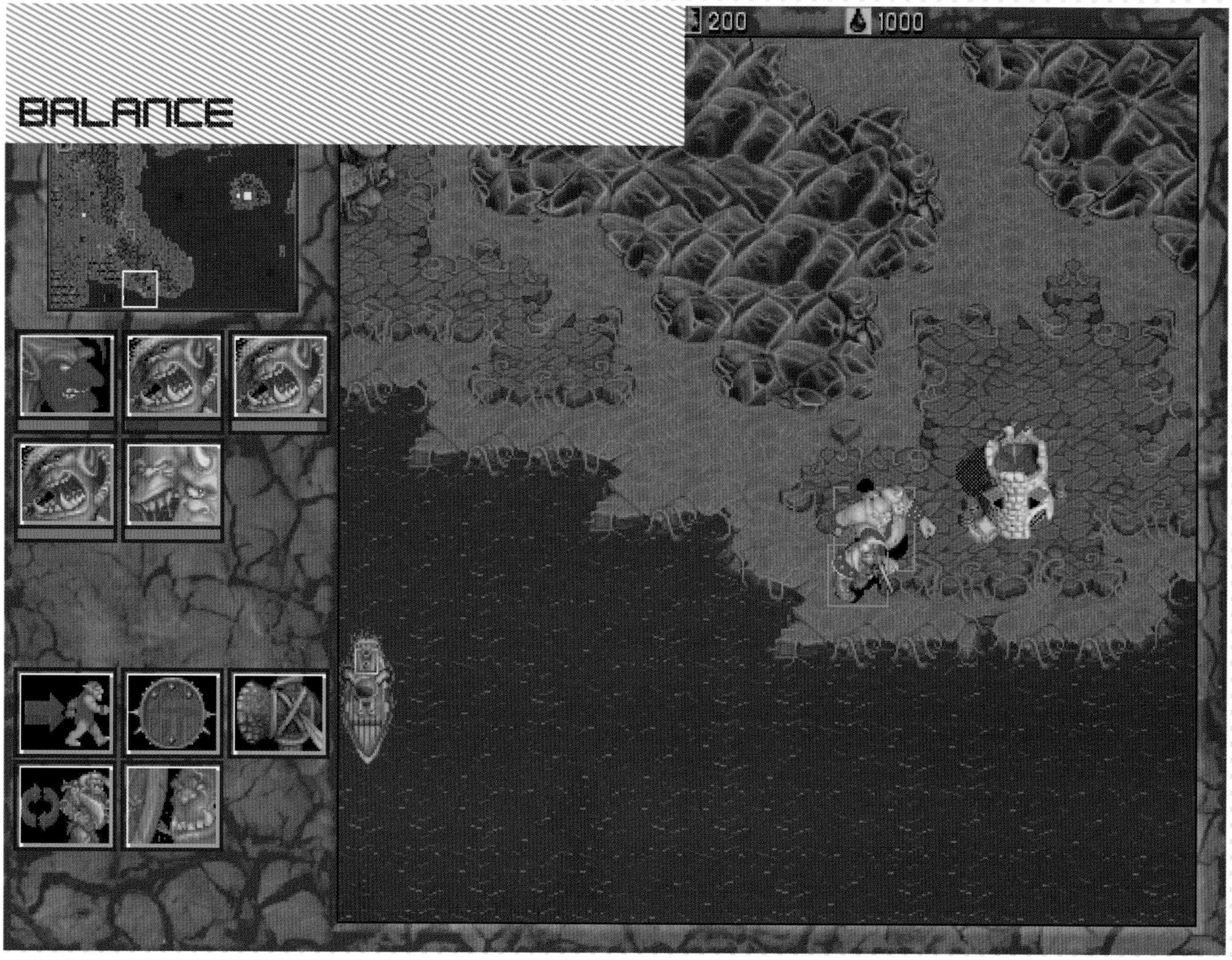

THERE ARE SEVERAL KINDS OF GAME BALANCE. FIRST THERE'S BALANCE AMONG THE RULES THEMSELVES. IS GOLD WORTH COLLECTING, GIVEN THE UNITS YOU CAN PRODUCE WITH IT? IS THE NUKE SO POWERFUL THAT EVERY OTHER WEAPON ISN'T WORTH BUILDING? AND SO ON.

Left: *Paladins and Ogre Mages in* ***Warcraft 2*** *have almost identical attributes. The main difference is that the Paladins can cast a healing spell whereas the Ogres are able to cast explosive runes. There isn't much difference most of the time. However, on a level consisting of many narrow mountain passes, the explosive runes gave the Ogres a real edge, because their explosive traps were unavoidable. This is not a flaw in the design. Balance doesn't guarantee that both sides will be equally matched on every terrain, only that the difference on some terrains will not make the game unwinnable.*

This is called static balance because it applies to the attributes and rules written into the design, which do not change with time. The designer can start tweaking his game for static balance even at the concept stage.

Particularly in strategy games, the designer will try to avoid dominant strategies. This requires some thought because of the fashion in RTS for 'races' with different abilities. *Warcraft 2* handled the problem of balance by having the two races (orc and human) functionally pretty much identical. The orc scouts flew zeppelins, for example, while the human scouts flew biplanes. The units looked different, so they gave a different flavour, but had the same stats.

In the case of *Warcraft 3*, Blizzard's designers had a bigger task. The races there are very different. They found the answer, and *Warcraft 3* is a well-balanced game with no obviously dominant units. But behind its apparently easy elegance must lie many hundreds of hours of testing and tweaking.

The other kind of balance, called dynamic because it applies in play, is more difficult for the designer to manage. It is possible to look at the problem qualitatively. For example, suppose that it is possible to capture and convert enemy soldiers. This is a positive feedback device. As one player starts winning, he'll increase the size of his army and then he'll win even faster.

That's not necessarily a bad game. The designer might be aiming for short battles where the game accelerates swiftly to victory when one player gets the upper hand. But it will throw out the balance between a novice and an experienced player. We, of course, expect the experienced player to do better. If it wasn't possible to get good at the game it would all just come down to luck. At the same time, positive feedback is not a forgiving game element. Usually it's better to have a game that lets a new player learn before he loses.

A more general extension of this aspect of balance is to make sure that effort is commensurate with reward. This is the way to ensure that the game finds the happy medium between triviality and impossibility!

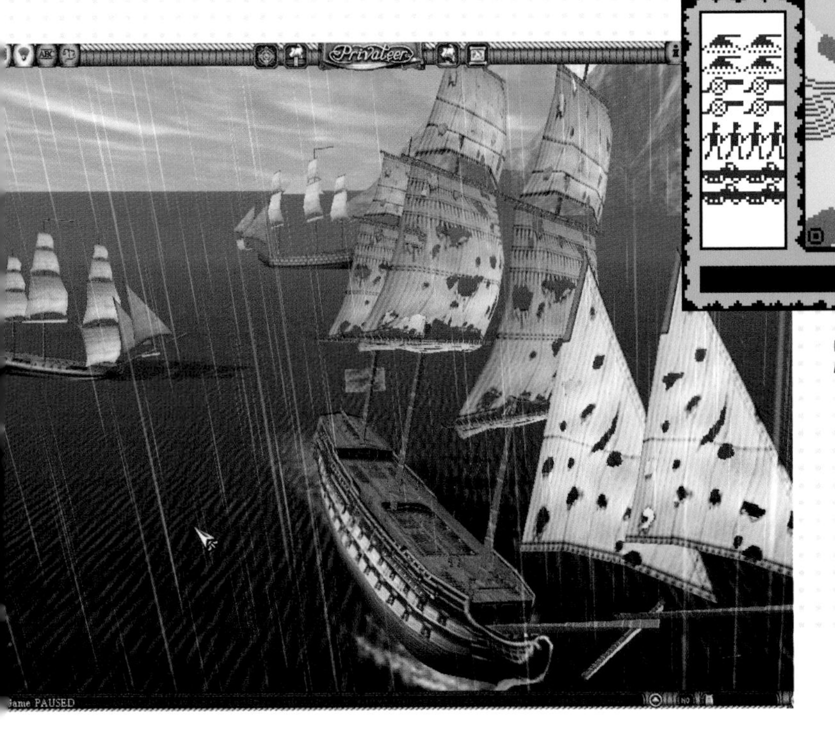

Left: ***Privateer's Bounty*** *by Akella.*

Above: *The fundamental issue of all game design is the balance of realism and playability. How far can you abstract the game world without sacrificing the sense of familiarity? Early games did well to coax what graphics they could from the machines of the day, as this screen from* ***Stonkers*** *shows. Now the issue is no longer what technology can deliver, but the sheer production time and cost.*

CAMPAIGNS AND LEVELS

CAMPAIGN STRUCTURE IN STRATEGY GAMES IS PRETTY MUCH ALWAYS HIGHLY DESIGNED. THAT IS, THE PLAYER STARTS EVERY FRESH LEVEL IN THE CAMPAIGN WITH UNITS AND RESOURCES THAT WERE CHOSEN BY THE DESIGNER, NOT BASED ON THE PLAYER'S ONGOING SUCCESS OVER A NUMBER OF LEVELS. THE OBVIOUS REASON WHY IT'S DONE THIS WAY IS THAT IT MAKES THE DESIGNER'S JOB SIMPLER.

All the same, the effect is intrusive because players rightly question why they won a huge battle in the last level and now have to start all over again with two tanks and a grunt.

'In a single-player game there needs to be controllable unfolding of experiences,' believes ***MARK ASHTON*** of Nicely Crafted Entertainment. 'The designer can draw a line under each mission and say exactly what units a player will have at that point. When you base the starting condition of a level on the exit conditions of the previous level, it's a problem because you are allowing the players to dig themselves into a hole.

'Those reservations aside, more freedom has proved to be very popular in other games, so I am sure there are good ways to implement it and retain control of the game experience.'

PAUL TWYNHOLM of Climax agrees. 'The potential exists to create a more freeform campaign structure but the baggage that comes with that should not be underestimated. The more parameters that can change between campaigns mean more design work, more balancing, more testing, etc. Also, as the unknowns increase outside each scenario, the scenarios need to be modified to accommodate the

Below: ***Chicago 1930*** *by Spellbound.*

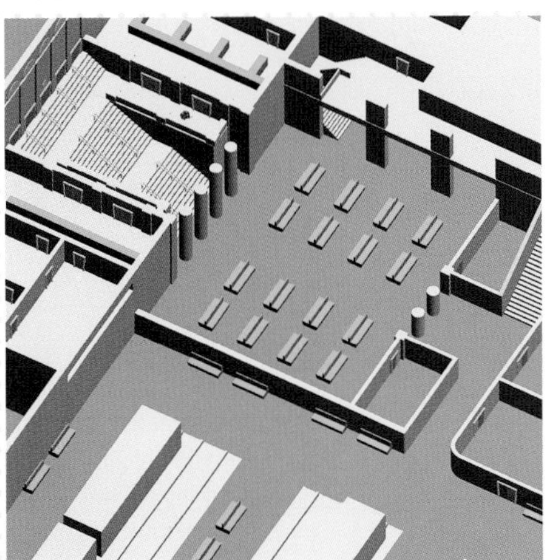

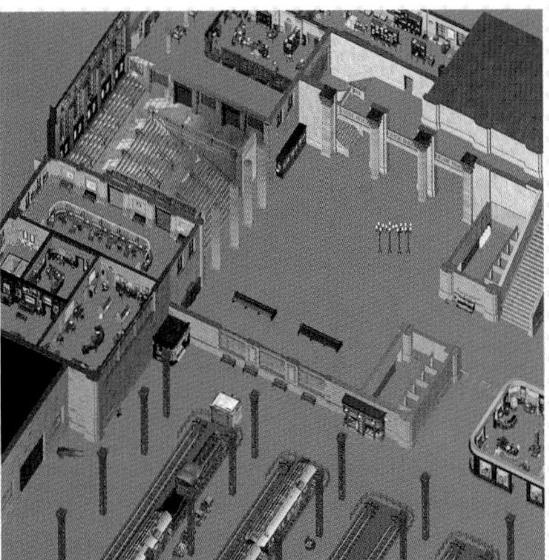

'For example, a player manages to complete level one but misses a useful crate that would have given him a more advanced tank. Level two he only just manages to complete – if he'd had the tank it would have been much easier – and so starts level three with just a handful of units. And still no advanced tank. In this case it isn't just a matter of restarting mission three, he will have to go back to mission one to make the most of the game.

Left: *Level design showcases different aspects of the underlying gameplay. For example, military formations are useful mainly on relatively open ground, so there is no point in designing a game with strong rules and an emphasis on formations if the levels are then all designed as a jumble of craters and hills. The level design of Independent Arts'* ***Against Rome*** *shows how it should be done.*

Right: ***Disciples*** *from Strategy First.*

CAMPAIGNS AND LEVELS 2

possibilities; this usually results in more generic scenario types. Up front I would be clear on what the design is trying to achieve. If the in-scenario mechanics are relatively generic (e.g. *Shogun Total War*) then you can afford to focus on the campaign. On the other hand, if you take something like *Command & Conquer* with a very rigid scenario structure, I would set less ambitious goals.'

For a truly strategic game, the ideal is for there to be no artificial delineation of levels. A large part of strategic warfare is picking the site of battle – here on the hills at Waterloo, not down the road in the valley at Charleroi. Players should be able to do that, not conform to the authorial designer's chosen scenario as we had to do (for very good reasons) in the days of boardgaming.

Generic (non-campaign) levels in ***Age of Empires*** *were created fractally from seed numbers, so that players never had the same map twice.*

In a perfect strategy wargame, the game environment would model the whole of Asia, say, and as Alexander the Great or Genghis Khan you'd fast-forward to the moments that interested you or demanded your attention – which hopefully would be the same thing. The 'levels' would be those moments where the general problem becomes specific, which in war is what we call a battle.

Instead of authoring the experience, the designer in such a game now becomes a transcendent deity, sculpting the landscape and bringing it to life with rules, but not even trying to anticipate all the stories that will be played out in that landscape.

The benefit is a truly user-owned experience. The risk is of the player reaching an impasse such as Mark Ashton described earlier: not picking up a vital upgrade. In a genuinely open game environment, the player has freedom to send units back and find that upgrade. A freeform environment doesn't mean the designer can't also include a watchful AI story-conductor that would note if something important had been overlooked and drop clues for the player. In a massively multiplayer strategy game, that role can, of course, be filled by other players. There will always be a market for information, and the market forces tend to conform to aesthetic story paradigms – whether it be the advice that comes in the nick of time to save the rich but crumbling old empire, or the advice that tragically came too late for the tiny struggling colony.

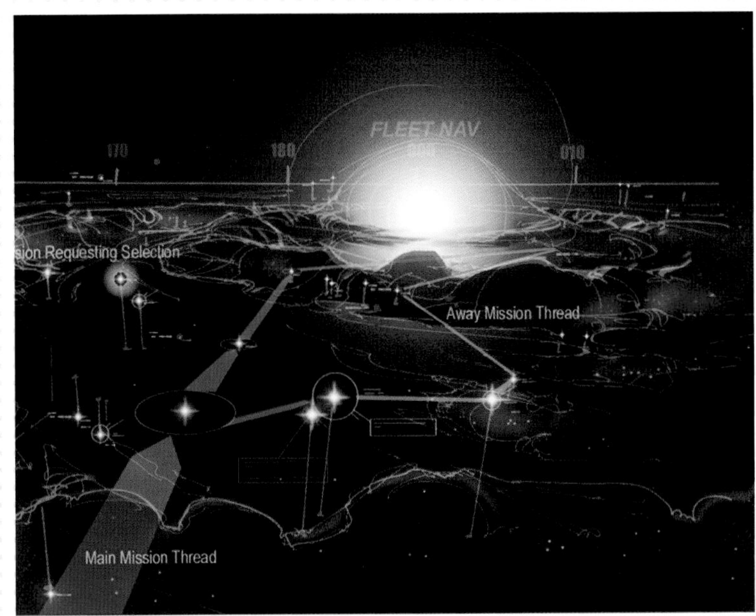

Homeworld 2 *by Relic.*

'THE PLAYER EXPECTS CERTAIN ELEMENTS FROM A STRATEGY GAME – RESOURCE GATHERING, EXPLORATION, EXPANSION. DESIGNERS HAVE TO CHOOSE. THEY EITHER SCALE DOWN THE AMOUNT OF RESOURCES TO KEEP THE MAP BALANCED AND ALLOW A BETTER PROGRESSION FROM MAP TO MAP; OR THEY SIMPLY HAVE THE PLAYER RESTART ON EVERY MAP, USING SOME PRETEXT SUCH AS NEW TERRITORY TO JUSTIFY IT. IN TIME, THE GENRE WILL EVOLVE INTO SOMETHING DIFFERENT AND WE'LL SEE NEW PROGRESSION SYSTEMS, SUCH AS CARRYING OVER YOUR ARMY FROM MAP TO MAP, OR HAVING A UNIQUE ARMY FOR THE WHOLE CAMPAIGN.'
DANNY BELANGER, DIRECTOR OF INTERNAL DEVELOPMENT AT STRATEGY FIRST

Left: ***Desperados*** *by Spellbound.*

*ENSEMBLE'S AGE SERIES OF STRATEGY GAMES HAS REVOLUTIONISED RTS GAMEPLAY AND NOW CLAIMS THE TOP SLOT IN THE GENRE. BUT WHEN **AGE OF EMPIRES** CAME OUT BACK IN 1998, THERE WAS NO ANY INITIAL EXPECTATION THAT IT WOULD BECOME THE BIGGEST OF THE RTS BRANDS. WHAT MADE IT KING OF THE RTS HILL?*

MARVEL OF THE AGE

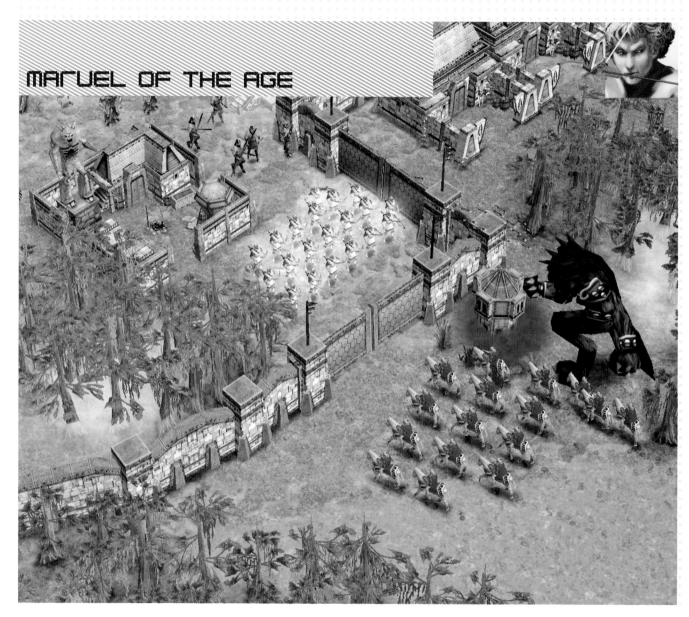

Above: ***Age of Mythology: The Titans.***

The genre had of course been around since *Dune 2*. Ostensibly all that Sandy Petersen and the developers at Ensemble were doing was putting that well-established gameplay into a context that was a little more grounded in reality. Players' partners – and in this genre at least that usually that means wives and girlfriends – can be fairly disdainful of 'geeky' fantasy and sci-fi games. The brilliance of the *Age* concept is that it's historically authentic; it feels respectable.

Each new release moves the *Age* series along. There were, for example, significant enhancements in the gameplay between the initial release of *Age of Empires* and its add-on pack, *Rise of Rome*.

Early RTS designers started out with the assumption that computer wargaming wouldn't be very different from the tabletop variety. So if you look at the different unit strengths in the original *Age of Empires* game, for example, you'll see that the armour, killing power and so on are just as a tabletop gamer would have them.

The interesting thing is that it didn't entirely work the way it was meant to. For example, players would use chariots a lot – far more than the historical use of chariots would imply – but pikemen just didn't prove to be worth spawning. To fix this, Ensemble tried reducing the population cost of pikemen in *Rise of Rome* – so now a player could have twice as many pikemen as anything else.

It was a patch but it still didn't much encourage players to use infantry. The key lay in the way units behaved. Archers' artificial intelligence allowed them to autotarget and concentrate fire, and chariots could reselect and get to new targets faster. In the absence of true formations, infantry weren't working as they should do in real life. That's why players weren't using them.

MARVEL OF THE AGE 2

Ensemble pored over the problem and had it fixed by the time *Age of Kings* came out. Now the game had behaviour protocols – meaning that you could set archers to skirmish, infantry could hold ground, and so on. Once the artificial intelligence had units acting as they would in a real battle, the unit attributes made sense.

It takes a lot of adjusting to get the different unit types balanced. The designers have to make a guess and hope they're in the right ballpark. Fortunately intuition seems to be fairly close to the mark. Even so, RTS designers end up adjusting behaviours and strengths considerably in playtesting.

To some extent it's self-balancing. If a particular unit, say a bombardier, is more useful than others then it gets used more. But the opponent also knows that. So, he will build more horsemen, because that's the unit that works best against bombardiers. The designers don't need to adjust all the spawning costs. That would be an ugly, messy way to handle it, and another characteristic of Ensemble's Age series is the cleanness of the design.

By the time of *Age of Mythology*, the designers have gone to great pains to make sure that units all have unique abilities. If a horseman is just a faster infantryman – the way it worked in the original *Age of Empires* – then you've got a problem. The answer lies in each unit doing different things. Scouts can cross mountains, infantry are strong in defence, chariots are fast but need level terrain, elephants smash down walls but are slow-moving, and so on. The concept of units not doubling up on function is sometimes called orthogonal attribute design. It means that there is enormous richness of gameplay waiting for the player to discover it.

In just a few years, Ensemble's Age series has risen to be regarded as the defining brand in the RTS game genre.

SCALE

*NO GENRE CALLS FOR SWEEPING SCALE SO MUCH AS STRATEGY. FOR THE AFICIONADO, EVEN EARTHBOUND EMPIRES AREN'T ALWAYS ENOUGH – FOR THE TRUE GRAND PLANNER IN THE HARI SELDON TRADITION, THERE ARE GALAXY-BUSTING SAGAS SUCH AS **HAEGEMONIA, HOMEWORLD** AND **EARTH & BEYOND.***

Above: ***Haegemonia: The Solon Heritage*** *from Digital Reality.*

Left: *Relic's* ***Homeworld 2.***

Down on the ground, the declared context of an epic game causes us to overlook the fact that the supposedly tremendous scale is often tantamount to a squabble between two neighbouring villages.

The processing power of the machines is now finally catching up with the possibilities inherent in 3D, potentially taking the next crop of strategy games to the grand strategic level.

But as the available space grows, what of time? On a realistic scale, military action above the operational level takes days even with 21st-century weaponry. When the legions of Rome can campaign again across virtual Europe, will gamers have the patience to go along for the march?

One solution is to alter the passage of time with the zoom level the player has chosen. In close-up, the player can adjust his battle formations and issue tactical orders just like any current RTS. As the view moves out, time speeds up. At this scale, legions are crossing continents in minutes and the player is making large-scale adjustments to his economy and building plans. In the event of engagement with the enemy, the view zooms back down and the player can decide whether to handle it personally or to zoom out and leave it to the AI generals.

It sounds good in theory, but strategic games in the past have done better to find their focus and stick to it. During design of *Gettysburg*, Sid Meier described his concerns about a game that would provide the player with both strategic and tactical levels. After zooming in and fighting a battle, the player could find that he'd lost sight of the bigger picture. Some players raised this complaint about *Tartan Army,* too.

And now we must consider the massively multiplayer aspect too. Variable time-rates aren't so manageable when you could have upwards of 100 players all with their own ideas of the best game speed at any one moment.

Possibly the answer to both issues is to create hierarchical games. Some players would be Churchill and Hitler, others Montgomery and Rommel, others the soldiers on the front line. It wouldn't even necessarily be the same game on all levels. A mobile game might determine the ammunition in a series of online first-person shooters (using the same game brand) that would decide the armaments used in a tactical battle game, whose outcome would set the units available at the strategic level.

'FROM A GAMEPLAY POINT OF VIEW, SCALE IS NOT AN ISSUE. LIKE IN TABLETOP, IF THERE ARE ENOUGH CHARACTERS AND CHARACTER TYPES PRESENT TO ALLOW GOOD GAMEPLAY, THE FACT THAT THEY REPRESENT ONE, FIVE, OR 500 UNITS BECOMES IRRELEVANT. WHERE IT DOES MATTER IS IN THE PLAYER'S PERCEPTION OF THE ENVIRONMENT. PLAYERS ARE USED TO THE SIZE AND SCALE OF STANDARD RTS GAMES AND IF THIS REMAINS THE SAME NOBODY IS LIKELY TO COMPLAIN. WITH ADVANCES IN TECHNOLOGY, HOWEVER, IT WILL BE POSSIBLE TO CREATE ENVIRONMENTS CLOSER TO WHAT CINEMAGOERS NOW EXPECT WHEN VIEWING MASS BATTLES IN FILMS LIKE ***LORD OF THE RINGS****. EVEN IF THE GAMEPLAY REMAINS THE SAME, THE BENCHMARK WILL BE RAISED AND NOBODY WILL EVER LOOK BACK.'*

PAUL TWYNHOLM, LEAD DESIGNER AT CLIMAX

REAL-TIME STRATEGY IS GETTING TO BE JUST LIKE A REAL BATTLE – SO MANY MEN THAT THEY JUST BECOME A VAST MARAUDING HORDE. THIS IS WAR ON A SCALE THAT THE EARLY RTS DEVELOPERS COULD ONLY DREAM OF. IN THOSE DAYS, JUST GETTING A FEW DOZEN SOLDIERS ON SCREEN AT ONE TIME MEANT SQUEEZING EVERY LAST OUNCE OF PROCESSING POWER OUT OF THE MACHINE.

IS BIGGER ALWAYS BETTER?

Above: ***Spellforce: The Order of Dawn*** *by Phenomic.*

Today Moore's Law means more, more, more. We waited so long for this that perhaps we're blinded to its faults. It doesn't necessarily deepen the experience to have all those troops. If the idea is that more lives at stake means more emotional impact, you can debunk that pretty quickly by considering Rourke's Drift or Thermopylae.

Look at films, which can depict battles involving thousands of men with relative ease. A decade or so back you could always hire an unemployed Eastern European army. Now with animation engines such as Weta used for the *Lord of the Rings* battle scenes it's even easier.

But does having all those heaving bodies on screen make a difference? Surely what matters is the moment that Sauron's finger is severed and the Ring falls to the ground. The million orcs and elves are just window-dressing to get your attention. Or consider the opening 20 minutes of

Above: *Elixir's simulation of a huge working city in* ***Republic: The Revolution****.*

Right: *Derring-do on the high seas in* ***Privateer's Bounty*** *from Akella.*

Right: ***Silent Storm*** *from Nival shows that interesting strategic complexity can also come from intricate detail on a small squad-based scale.*

Saving Private Ryan – spectacular, but it's the simple, mortal struggle of two men in the upstairs room of a bombed-out house that we remember.

And if you do have thousands of men in your game, how is the player going to control them? Thousands of troops are hard to manage. That's why war rooms throughout the world show whole battalions as a single icon on a map. You can surround blocks of units with coloured ident bubbles – but in that case, so much for the quest to create a realistic depiction of the battlefield.

Alternatively you could have troops assigned to battalion tabs that the player selects to issue orders. That means directing the battle the way it works in real life – through the chain of command. That's better than painting around units to select them Windows-style, but it still leaves you gazing down from an altitude of 1000 feet, unmoved by the turbulence on the bestial floor. Worse still, you might find players effectively preferring to spend most of their time in a simpler, 2D iconic display and hardly bothering with the photorealistic, trillion-polygon engine you're so proud of.

There is little point in strategy games chasing realism, in terms of the size of levels or the numbers of personnel, if the consequence of that extra scale is to force the use of an intrusive or abstract interface. The designer's aim must be to deliver the feeling of strategic scale combined with immersion and simplicity.

'THOUSANDS OF TROOPS!' CRIES THE BLURB. ***'LEVELS AS BIG AS A PACIFIC ISLAND! BATTLES THAT PLAY OUT OVER DAYS!'***

STYLE

MANY WILL REMEMBER THE ROOTS OF STRATEGY GAMING: HUNDREDS OF CARDBOARD BUTTONS THAT BLOW AWAY LIKE LEAVES SHOULD ANYONE SNEEZE; HUNDREDS OF HOURS, EYES STRAINING, TO PAINT COSTLY METAL MINIATURES; AND YET MORE HUNDREDS OF CARDS, FANCY DICE AND PLASTIC MARKERS THAT ARE INEVITABLY LOST IN THE CARPET OR CHEWED BY THE DOG.

This 3D physicality has translated itself in the 2D medium of the computer game. The goal in computer gaming has always been to provide some kind of 3D representation of the battlefield, even before real-time 3D engines became available to the genre. It has practical uses in that the battlefield can be rotated and zoomed as though peering at toy soldiers on a tabletop.

However, it can also confuse and obscure and requires an understanding of the manipulation of 3D space in a computer that is often alien to a novice. The real attraction of the 3D representation is its physicality. We want to reach into the screen and pick up the little wriggling soldiers and feel the satisfying weight of them in our hand. Apart from a very few exceptions, all modern computer strategy is now based on 3D representation and is stylistically guided from the point of view of a model maker or sculptor rather than a 2D illustrator.

It is critical in today's crowded and frenetic market to find a visual style that gives a game an identity in the mind of the player. This styling derives from two mutually dependent elements. The first must be content – the world the game is depicting. Games based on imaginary worlds enjoy almost total freedom and can use character design, architectural invention and even the topography of a fantasy landscape to create marketable properties.

Left: ***Massive Assault*** *by Wargaming.net has a bright, chunky style as though you are playing with robust toys.*

Below: *Paradox's* ***Crusader Kings*** *has created a complete style that seems redolent of Regency clubrooms and wargames played by gaslight.*

Below left: *Blizzard's* ***Warcraft*** *series has always had a strong semi-cartoon style, which gives it a distinctive identity.*

Far left: *Elixir's* ***Evil Genius*** *revisits the swinging sixties with a dash of souped-up postmodern style.*

Left: ***Africa Korps vs. Desert Rats*** *by Digital Reality has a very solid three-dimensional quality, almost more real than reality.*

STYLE 2

There have been a number of examples in computer gaming of truly original vision. But, sadly, many game designers squander the opportunity, preferring constantly to refer back to what have become over-used clichés from Hollywood and the games industry itself. It's a tough call. Original ideas, particularly those that lie at the edge of common experience, can turn gamers off, leaving the title to languish in obscurity.

Historical games have a pre-defined world from which to gather their imagery and must therefore rely almost entirely on the second element, of superficial style, to stand out. Superficial style is the way that the game is graphically represented. Consider the distinction between the realism of ducks on a pond painted by Constable and the graphic cartoon world of Donald Duck, with millions of variations between.

A game can be represented in any one of these styles, each giving a different tone to how the player perceives the gameplay style. A game that peers through a dirty lens just feet from the grime on the street leads one to expect grim, squad-level action of bayonets and bouncing grenades. View sparkling seas, verdant rolling hills and snow-topped peaks from cloudless sky, and you'd expect to command great armies of colour-bedecked knights from one spired city to another. Perhaps the most difficult historical period to depict in a marketably distinct way is WWII. Depicting Hitler's finest in the levity of a cartoon style is simply tasteless – though tastelessness has not always been a concern of the games industry.

Above: *Game setups in* ***Disciples II*** *by Strategy First are great excuses to display wonderfully evocative artwork.*

Right: ***Gettysberg*** *by Firaxis. The charming and functional graphics are reminiscent of tabletop gaming.*

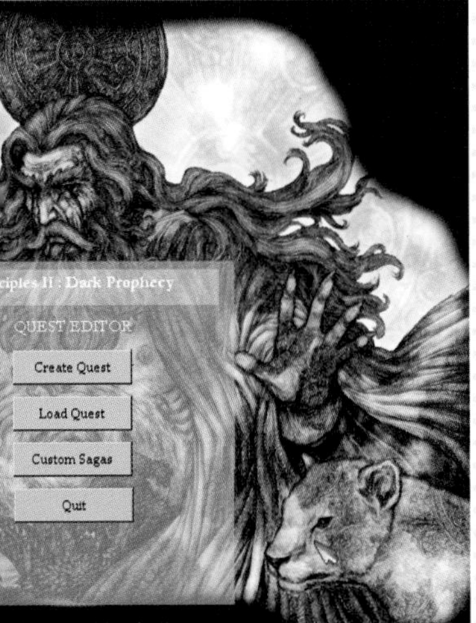

With the constant improvement in graphics hardware, a large part of the games industry has been on a relentless march towards realism, which is what one would expect in such a young medium. Realism prevails in strategy as in any other genre but with interesting variations caused by the influence of the genre's roots in tabletop gaming, and the necessities of clarity in gameplay. Typically, although intricately detailed and rendered, units are modelled too large for their environment. Soldiers are seen looking into the first-floor windows of their diminutive houses while tanks crunch through forests of Bonsai. If correctly scaled, buildings would take up too much of the screen and you would quickly lose units in the long grass. The human figure is also drawn differently – stockier, with large hands and exaggerated insignia – helping you see characters and identify them. It is an example of style over substance, because players would be better served with flat, numbered icons if pure gameplay was the only objective.

The truth is that visuals are easily as important as gameplay in the commercial world. The graphics help create a believable game environment that transports the player beyond the strategy itself. Some recent games are so beautifully illustrated that they become works of art in themselves, and the player can get as much from the graphics as from gameplay. It is, however, an unequal balance. Such graphics are increasingly expensive as production values begin to rival those of blockbuster films. Gameplay itself rarely receives the same investment.

GAMEPLAY

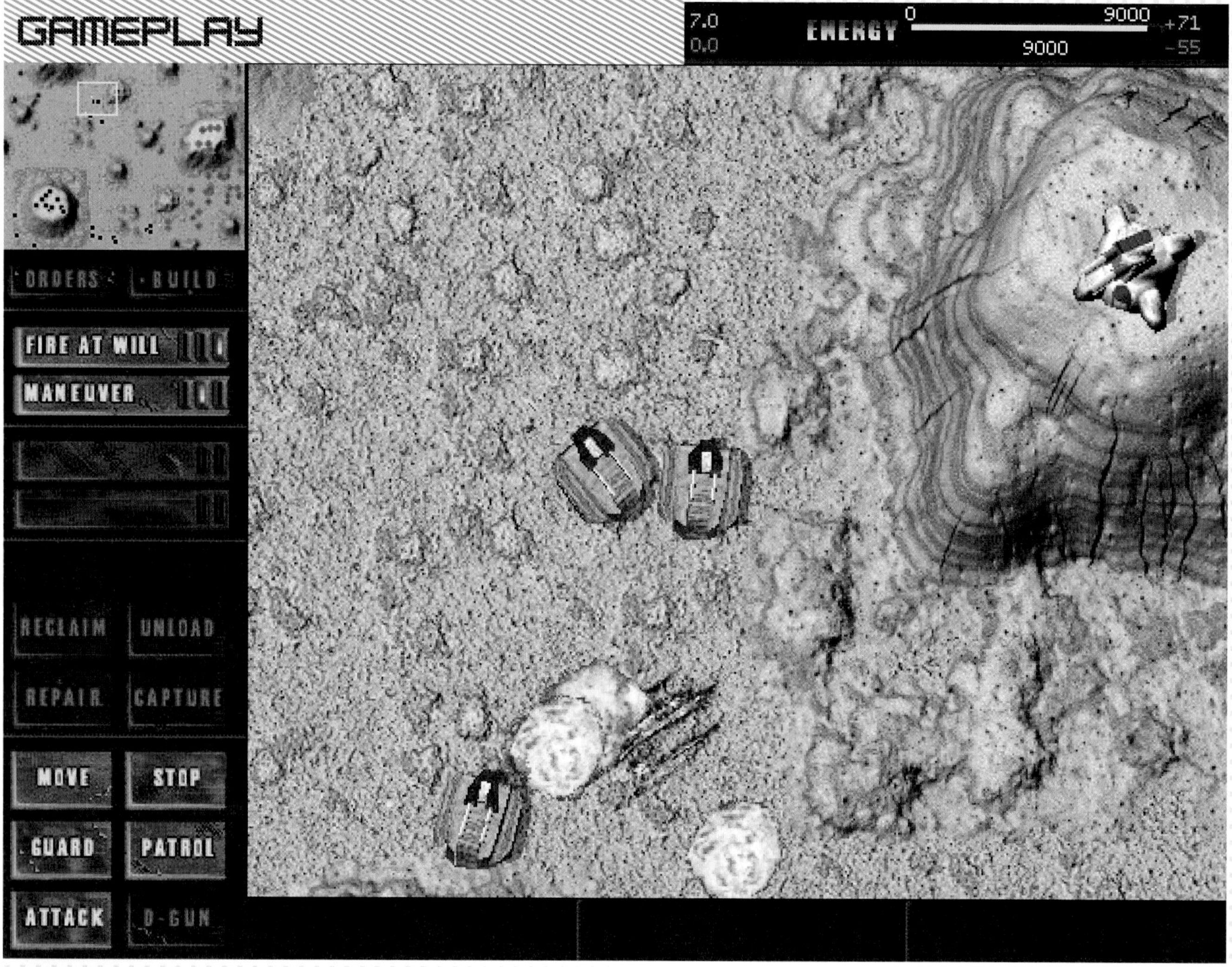

GAMEPLAY IS A WORD OFTEN USED BUT RARELY DEFINED. SID MEIER OFFERED ONE DEFINITION THAT HAS BEEN WIDELY QUOTED: 'GAMEPLAY IS A SERIES OF INTERESTING CHOICES'.

*Scripted gameplay poses a problem specifically set by the designer of the game. For example, this level from **Total Annihilation** by Cavedog required the player to fulfil the specific objective of destroying the blue base. More commonly among current real-time games, the designer only poses the generic problem in the form of an environment, a set of rules and an opponent. A wilderness of authorial intent is Paradise now!*

'A GOOD PLAN EXECUTED TODAY IS BETTER THAN A PERFECT PLAN EXECUTED AT SOME INDEFINITE POINT IN THE FUTURE.' GEORGE PATTON

Top: *The brave new world of **Impossible Creatures** by Relic.* Above: ***Space Colony** by Firefly.*

When we use the term 'gameplay' in the Game Guru series, we don't mean it to include every aspect of a game. The setting, theme and style are quite different things. When we slice down dozens of foes in *Dynasty Warriors*, or race along the walls in *Prince of Persia: Sands of Time*, those choices are not the gameplay Sid Meier spoke of. They're fun.

Gameplay choices are fun, too, but it's a more cerebral kind of pleasure. Do I invest in biotech stocks, which could go through the roof but probably won't, or in a tracker fund giving me a far more certain reward but little hope of a big payoff? Or should I keep my savings in the bank in case there's a stock market crash? And the bank might go out of business, so would I be wiser to buy krugerrands and keep them under my bed?

Those are interesting choices because they all have an upside and a downside. There's no simple solution. There may not even be any 'right' answer. You're balancing current considerations at the same time as looking ahead to how your choices now will kick off a whole set of further choices. You're trying to manage those choices to bring the whole system into a state that can be described as victory – either in comparison with another player, or by reference to agreed victory conditions.

AND THAT IS WHAT WE CALL GAMEPLAY

No game consists only of gameplay. Even chess and Go, which if found in a box by an alien visitor to our world would certainly be described as pure games, in fact bring other connotations to the experience. Look around any Go player's home. Usually you'll find a Japanese lacquered vase or a paper screen, if not a set of Mizoguchi DVDs. The game player is not immune to romance any more than the rest of us.

Modern computer games are costly mass-market entertainment products and they have to offer us more than just interesting choices, more than gameplay alone. Even the strategy genre – one of the 'purest' forms – needs cool particle effects, captivating characters, and a setting that grabs the player's imagination.

'IN WAR, MORALE ACCOUNTS FOR THREE-QUARTERS, THE BALANCE OF ACTUAL FORCES ONLY FOR ONE QUARTER.' NAPOLEON BONAPARTE

PSYCHOLOGY, THOUGH A MAJOR FACTOR IN REAL WARFARE, IS RARELY PART OF STRATEGY WARGAMES...

THE WAR INSIDE

Above: ***Deactivation*** *by Akella.*

Consider the paradigm of knights versus footmen in medieval warfare. This depends on two factors. First, horses will not charge through a massed line of men in good order. Horses are stupid, but most aren't that stupid. They can see that in the resulting pile-up of bodies they have a good chance of falling or breaking a limb.

Second, a line of footmen drawn up against a line of knights fighting toe to hoof, as it were, gives the advantage to the footmen. They have greater concentration of killing power along the line, as men can fight shoulder to shoulder while the knight needs room to manouevre and swing his sword. Moreover, the footmen can place spears or pikes for thrusting up with more force.

Above: ***Cossacks: European Wars*** *from GSC Game World*

Top: *Firefly's* ***Stronghold*** *measures happiness among your populace. But you can't please all of the people all of the time, and in fact the player can ignore happiness altogether and just apply the stick.*

So in general, a group of knights facing a group of organised men in line will lose. But there are ways around this. Imagine that instead of charging those footmen in a line, the knights form up into a wedge formation. Now, as the footmen see the knights thundering towards them, there will be a point when the footman in the middle looks into the eyes of the leading knight and starts to feel he would be just a little bit safer if he moved to the left or right. A moment later, his subconscious performs the same calculation regarding the knight he's now facing in the second row of the wedge. So he shuffles a bit further to the left. Meanwhile, the footman to that footman's left is doing the same thing – while the man on his other side is shuffling nervously to the right.

The result is that even a well-trained line of footmen will split in confusion, giving victory to the knights. You can imagine it as a 'threat radius' that extends out ahead of the wedge and effectively pushes the line of footmen apart before the knights even reach them. And it works because it affects the footmen on a subconscious level. Their training doesn't help.

'TWO ARMIES ARE TWO BODIES OF MEN THAT MEET AND TRY TO FRIGHTEN EACH OTHER.'

NAPOLEON BONAPARTE

THE WAR INSIDE 2

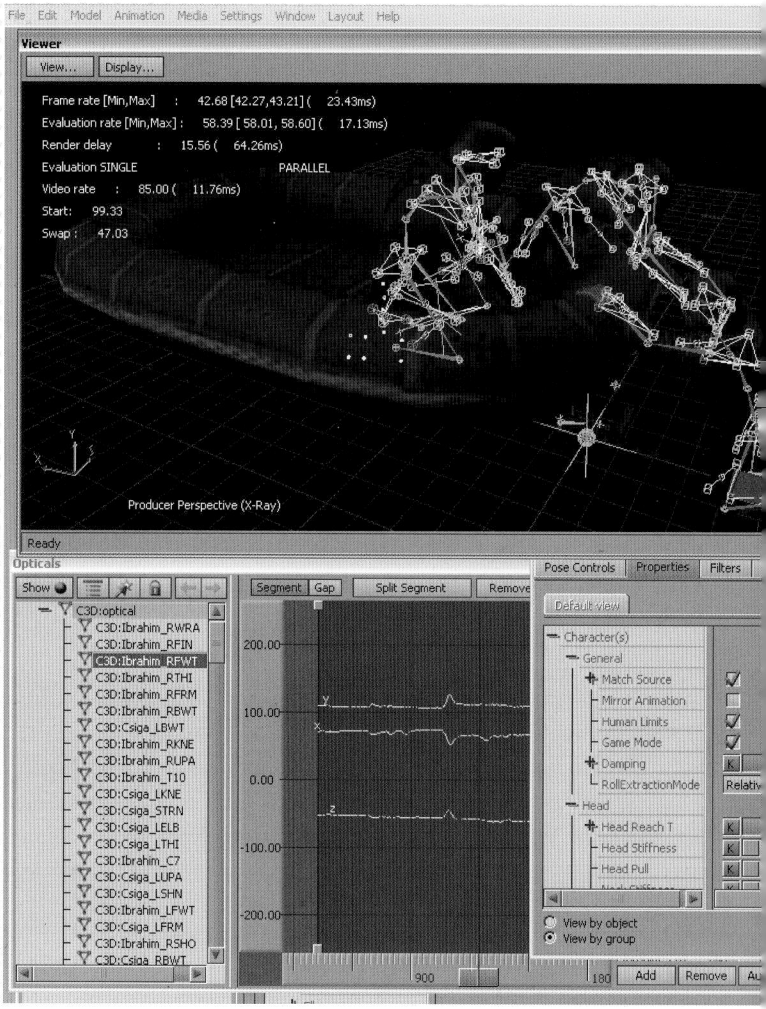

KEEP IT IN PLAIN SIGHT

Now, you wouldn't use threat radii in an RTS. Why not? Because they violate one of the fundamental rules of real-time gaming. The player can't see a threat radius, and suddenly having his men break and run because of a hidden effect isn't acceptable.

But the times they are a-changing, and rules are meant to be broken. Today we can depict the psychological dimension of war. Games are lavishing more effort on sound and animation. So, instead of mysteriously parting those footmen like Moses on the Red Sea, you'd hear the roaring and screaming as the knights came pounding in. You'd see the frightened shuffling of the footmen, hear their intakes of breath, watch their shoulders wilt and their knees sag.

Well, maybe. It's a high-budget game that can afford to go into that level of detail. And yet the bar is rising. Players demand a deeper experience, and morale is one way to deliver that. The tricky part is making sure that it's clearly visible – and we don't mean with cheesy effects like 'fear bubbles' over characters' heads!

TERROR TACTICS

The term 'swashbuckling' comes from the Anglo-Saxon warriors who used to strike (swash) their shields (bucklers) to create a truly terrifying din. It's the same principle as Maori warriors performing a haka. After watching that, enemies should know better than to mess with them. When you have overwhelming odds, an intimidating show of strength can be enough to send the smaller force running from the field.

Codename: Panzers from CDV Software. The sophistication of game graphics and animation brings more reality to the polygons flickering across our screens. Will games get so good that we really feel the fear our forebears felt arriving at the front line? The question may seem specious, but if television programmes like the BBC's Dunkirk retrospective can move us, then why shouldn't games?

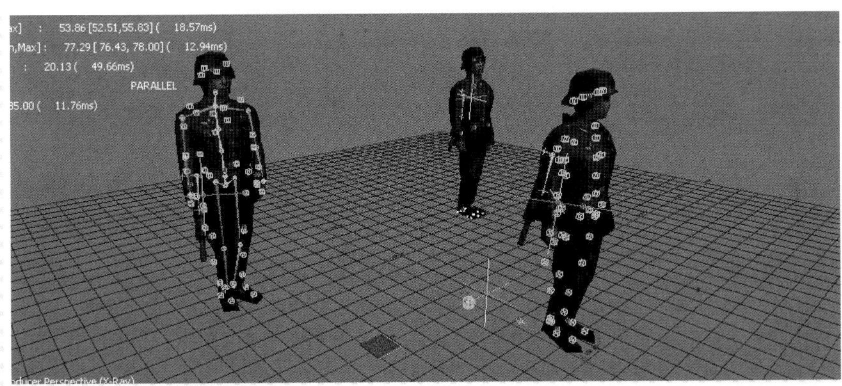

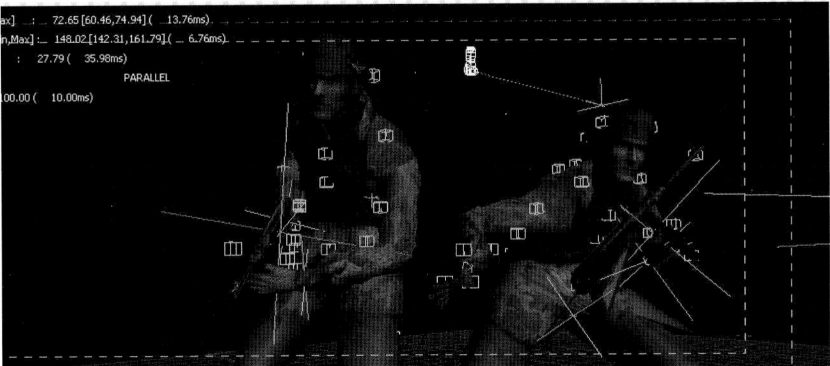

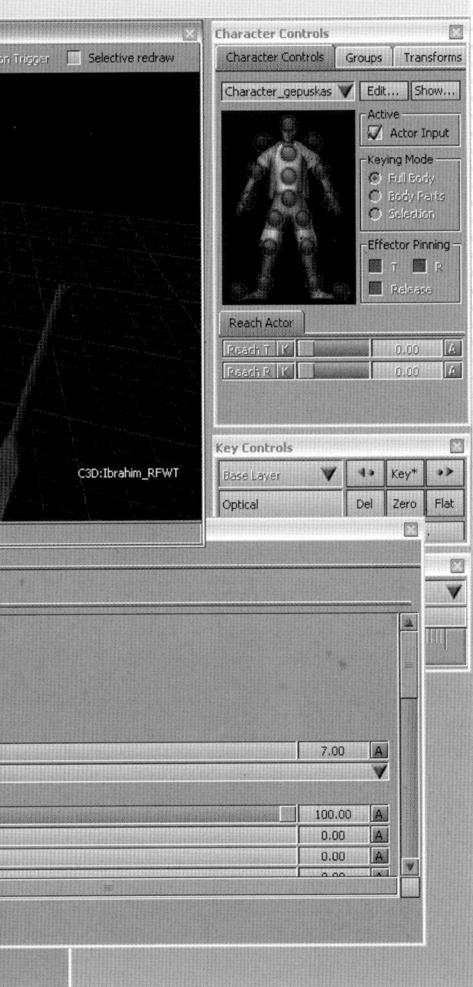

Assuming your game has the resources to portray morale effects convincingly, they can really enhance the gameplay. Fear puts the pressure on! It means you can't just leave formations standing untended like so many tabletop models. The moment you bring men into the front line, they start to become involved in the pre-melée exchange of insults, threats and jeers. You'll have to be sure to back up those footmen so they feel secure – if they're looking pale and knock-kneed now, just wait until the enemy berserkers start shouting at them.

Morale emphasises the value of veteran troops, who should be less likely to break and rout. (Although having said that, consider the Old Guard at Waterloo.) It adds a tense extra dimension to RTS warfare – when you bring men into danger, you'd better use them or lose them. And morale means you won't spend the game fighting lots of pointless uneven skirmishes. If one side is outclassed, it will retreat until it feels safe.

If morale suits the game and you have the development budget to carry it off palpably, then include it. But don't hide it among a bunch of invisible equations because that just serves to annoy the players.

SETTINGS

THE SETTING FOR A STRATEGY GAME RARELY COMES UNDER MUCH SCRUTINY. THE DECISION IS MORE OFTEN MADE FROM THE HEART. IT'S A PLACE AND TIME YOU JUST WANT TO PLAY.

Above: *The city that never sleeps.* ***Vegas: Make it Big*** *by Deep Red.*

DANNY BELANGER, *Director of Internal Development at Strategy First, talks about* ***Disciples II: The Dark Prophecy*** *(right): 'Strategy will most likely blend with other genres. For example, the* ***Disciples*** *series was one of the first strategy games to contain many features traditionally associated with role-playing games: gaining levels, hero skills, paperdoll-item management. Many games now have similar elements. I think the strategy genre will evolve in many interesting ways: online grand wars or multilayered strategic management.'*

Historical settings are ostensibly the simplest. Everything is defined for the designer, from the architecture to the relative strength of bow strings. It is simply a matter of gathering and sorting the material. However, historical gamers can be very exacting and have huge stores of knowledge extending right down to the smallest detail, making them formidable critics should the designer fail to meet their exacting standards.

Of course, history can be written to give a multitude of different versions and the same goes for gameplay. Some wargames are accurate recreations of battles down to the starting positions of every footman and bugler, but the evolution of the RTS has produced the concept of generic history where all the individual elements are correct – you just mix and match them any way you want.

Perhaps the most popular periods are medieval and World War II. Knights with their fluttering standards and glinting armour are an obvious attraction, but this period also offers an interesting mix of units: cavalry, archers, siege engines and castle defences in battles that are on a manageable scale. Hastings and Agincourt are fields you can run across, whereas the battles of a millennium earlier or a half-millennium later involve many tens of thousands of men.

There is a grim attraction to World War II. We can picture ourselves on the front line by just rewinding a couple of generations, and the struggle to overthrow the Nazis gives a clear enemy. Twentieth-century warfare is often played at a tactical or squad level, the sheer scale of true strategic level play being too much for any armchair general.

Fantasy and sci-fi also make perfect settings for wargaming because the conflicts can be reduced to good and evil, matter and anti-matter, law and chaos. Perhaps the most difficult aspect of this genre is to bring something fresh to the hard drive in place of the predictable hordes of orcs, goblins and elves or sci-fi's tired rehashing of space opera.

Strategy can still find new, fresh fields of battle, too. *Rapscallions*, a game based on the antics of gangs of kids, is a good example. The units are the kids themselves: the short-sighted guy with his chemistry set making stink bombs; the rangy kid with his fast knobbly-kneed gait; the big bully ready to hand out Chinese burns; the tomboy scampering up trees to scout. Weapons range from insults, mud-slinging and food-fights to catapults. Resources are pockets full of conkers and string, and the time left before Mum calls you in for dinner, while treehouses are forts to be defended and go-carts become chariots to be ridden into battle. Victory goes to the gang who send their enemy home crying with scraped knees and grass in their hair. As so many children's books have shown, the imagination of a child has room for everything from pirates to spaceships. If you can't fight a war in the Balkans, a scrap in the playground can be just as dramatic.

SETTINGS 2

Opposite page
Top left: *Another kind of American dream gets explored in* ***1503 AD: The New World*** *from Sunflowers.*

Top right: *Looks like one cold war in Pyro's classic* ***Commandos 3.***

Right: *Human history collides with Harryhausen in* ***BC****, Intrepid's game of tribe-building in the dawn of Man.*

Left: *Gunfight at the OK Corral in* ***Desperados 2*** *from Spellbound.*

*IN **GANGLAND**, FROM DANISH DEVELOPER MEDIAMOBSTERS, THE PLAYER IS PART OF A CRIME FAMILY WHO HAVE COME TO PARADISE CITY, USA, FROM SICILY TO CARVE OUT A NEW EMPIRE AMONG THE RACKETS.*

MEAN STREETS

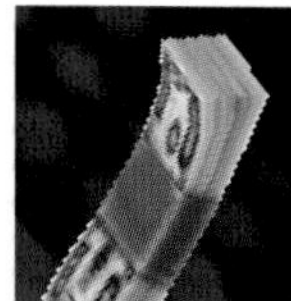

The overhead zoomed-out view and mouse-click control system place *Gangland* squarely in the RTS genre, but under the bonnet the game has features that blend across other styles of play to create something genuinely new and interesting – a stylish and original take on the cutting edge of 'RPS'.

MediaMobsters promise a new kind of non-linear RTS game where you can 'bribe, steal, kill, bootleg, seduce, put out contracts, make drive-by hits, and blow up buildings'. The action plays out against the backdrop of a living city where you can interact with over 500 non-player characters, each with his or her individual motivations and behaviours.

Key events are cued to happen at specific points for dramatic effect, but the way that each game plays out is different every time. What you do as player affects the way that NPCs will react. This and the small number of units gives the game something of a freeform role-playing feel, but the scope is strategic, with emphasis on the accumulation of resources, connections and even establishing a crime dynasty through alliance and marriage.

WE SPOKE TO ***ADAM GREGERSON****, CO-FOUNDER OF MEDIAMOBSTERS, ABOUT THE COMPANY'S FRESH ANGLE ON STRATEGY AND WHERE HE SEES THEM GOING NEXT.*

Strategy has come to be synonymous with real time. Is there still a place for the old turn-based strategy games that gave you unlimited time to ponder a decision?

AG: What game you prefer in any given situation I think depends on your mood and how much time you've got. Opening a good bottle of red wine when everybody else is asleep and playing a well executed turn-based or slow-paced RTS game can be just as satisfying as sharing a six-pack with the guys and tearing each other to shreds in a chaotic FPS.

All pictures: *Sharp suits, sleazy clubs and Sicilian proverbs abound in the atmospheric rackets-based strategy game* ***Gangland****, from Mediamobsters.*

MEAN STREETS 2

Building a base and economy, exploring the unknown, or commanding an army in battle – which of these game elements, if any, is the heart of strategy gaming?
AG: I've always mostly enjoyed the consolidation phase of RTS games and not so much the actual conflict. Of course, it wouldn't be as much fun building a base and collecting resources if that constant thought of being overrun by your opponents' forces wasn't there in the back of your head. But sometimes when I get hammered, I just feel like shouting, 'Hey I'm not ready yet!' As soon as I lose my most important structures and units, I also lose faith and can't wait to build up a new army. And then it happens all over again...

Is there a future on consoles for the RTS genre?
AG: Of course. There's a mouse and keyboard for console. The TVs are getting better with higher resolutions, and the couch is certainly a fine place from which to conquer new civilisations. It won't be long before we'll see a dramatic rise in RTS games for consoles, I think.

Where next for strategy games?
AG: With *Gangland*, MediaMobsters has tried to mix some new ingredients into the traditional RTS game. You have fewer units (RPG), more interaction with the environment (action), and a living milieu (sim). This creates different gameplay opportunities, although at heart it's still an RTS game. I think that developers will try to invent new spices and change the RTS games into a less linear experience. Some of the RTS games I've tried lately are no more than graphically enhanced versions of *Age of Empires* and *Red Alert* which I think isn't fair, as games do cost a lot of money.

All pictures: *Fast-paced action, role-playing elements and a living criminal underworld put **Gangland** apart from more conventional titles in the strategy genre.*

THE PLAYING EXPERIENCE

Which do you personally find more interesting in the trade-off between the emotional and cerebral experience of strategy? That is, how it actually feels to be a commander as distinct from the kinds of decisions a commander has to make.

AG: I believe the rocket science of making a good RTS game is enabling the commander to make interesting decisions. In a racing game or an FPS it's much more about the feeling, but RTS games are more thoughtful. The kinds of questions the player is asking are 'Should I build this structure or should I spend my money on this upgrade?'

Is it essential that the player is the commander in chief? Can you envisage a workable strategy game where the player is Ney rather than Napoleon?

AG: Maybe. Especially if at some point you could kick the Bonaparte butt and take over his operation – which in turn I guess would make you commander in chief. So, as in any game, finishing in second place probably just isn't good enough to satisfy most players.

MEAN STREETS 3

THE GAME WORLD

Terrain hasn't really played a major part in strategy gameplay in the past. Is that because of the genre's roots in tabletop wargames and boardgames where terrain often has only an 'overlay' effect?

AG: Well, I remember standing on a hill and throwing grenades in the face of everybody who tried to mess up my outfit back in the good old *Red Alert* days. Other RTS games have used terrain and environment, but it's true that it has been to a limited degree. In *Gangland* we've really tried to get the environment in play. You can take cover behind anything in the city. We haven't got terrain as such, but we'll definitely implement that in the sequel as it adds an extra dimension to both visceral appeal and gameplay.

Will better graphics and physics allow terrain and other environmental effects like weather, etc., to have a greater role in games?

AG: Definitely. As our eyes and our minds become more and more demanding, any developer making RTS, FPS, RPG or any other type of game will have to try to constantly break the limit of what's possible to create a great visual and gameplay experience.

Napoleon said that real war was mainly a matter of luck and morale. Both of those are hard to represent in a game. Should designers try, or do RTS gamers prefer a 'cleaner' kind of challenge?

AG: Luck should play a very limited role in an RTS game I think. The whole idea is for players to compete on equal footing and both good and bad luck would spoil that.

In boardgames and tabletop wargaming, each counter or figure represents many men. In a computer game, we think of each figure as one man – which implies Alexander fighting his battles on the scale of a football pitch. Does this matter?

AG: I recall reading that Alexander wept as he surveyed his empire because there was nothing left to conquer. Reducing Alexander's army to a boy scout gathering wouldn't tell the true story, and as such it certainly would matter. There have been quite a few good RTS games with thousands of units to tell the true story of those ancient epic battles.

All pictures: ***Gangland*** *brings a more interactive environment into play. If you can see it, you can take cover behind it.*

THE FUTURE

GAMES ARE BIG BUSINESS – NOT AS BIG AS HOLLYWOOD, WHATEVER YOU MAY HAVE READ, BUT BIG ALL THE SAME, AND GETTING BIGGER. EVEN WITH ALL THE HYPE AND HYPERBOLE STRIPPED AWAY, THE PRODUCTION COST OF A TRIPLE-A TITLE CAN CLEAR $10 MILLION.

When publishers start spending that kind of money, it's bound to have a knock-on effect on the creative side. Like all entertainment industries, games are hit-driven. A few massive successes pay for all the flops. In a situation like that, people start looking for guarantees. Feng shui, astrology, or marketing theories – anything that lets you believe you have a little bit of steer away from failure.

Rewind a decade or so. Games cost a lot less to make and so there was room for diversity. It's like looking at the Burgess shale fossils. All those wondrous and hallucinogenically strange creatures reduced finally to just a few established body forms – or genres, as we call them in entertainment.

Left: ***Savage: The Battle for Newerth*** *by S2 Games.*

Below: ***Silent Storm*** *by Nival Interactive.*

The positive side of this process is that game designers need to recognise the whole range of skills needed to entertain a mass audience. You aren't going to see carnivorous toilet bowls or strategy games about running a village fair.

The negative side is the emphasis on me-too. Many of 2004's crop of World War II games are very good, but the reason they exist is because Mr Spielberg chose to follow *Saving Private Ryan* with *Band of Brothers*. After *Troy* and *Alexander*, expect the strategy games of 2008 to be a long string of ancient epics.

Where next for strategy games? The management genre has already given rise to *The Sims* – a game that thinks it's a management sim but is really the start of something much more interesting. Strategic problems don't have to be large-scale, they only have to be wide-ranging and compelling.

It would be possible for example to have a strategy game based on the old TV programme *Rawhide*. You have to keep your herd together and drive them up the Chisholm trail, at the same time scouting ahead, surviving in the wild, and managing the relationships within your team. The strategy comes mostly from the personalities involved – the rest of it is the equivalent of resource gathering.

Right now, no publishing executive would give the go-ahead that concept – and quite rightly, because nobody is out looking through the boxes at Sam Goody for a *Rawhide* game. But it would be a different story if ever the Western makes a comeback because, in entertainment here at the start of the 21st century, it's still Hollywood that is calling the shots.

But maybe not for much longer. Games, after all, have only just got started.

'STORIES IN GAMES WILL BECOME MORE AND MORE STANDARD. DESIGNERS WILL TRY TO IMPLEMENT BETTER STORIES. IT IS POSSIBLE TO CREATE OPEN-ENDED STORIES AND STILL BE INTERESTING. THE MAIN TOOL TO BE USED IS CHOKE POINTS. THE PLAYER CAN GO WHEREVER HE LIKES, BUT IN TIME HE WILL BE FORCED TO PASS BY A SPECIFIC POINT. THAT CHOKE POINT IS WHERE THE DESIGNER CAN INTEGRATE STORY ELEMENTS OR CHARACTER GROWTH.'
DANNY BELANGER, DIRECTOR OF INTERNAL DEVELOPMENT AT STRATEGY FIRST

A WORLD OF DIFFERENCE

***TOBY SIMPSON**, MANAGING DIRECTOR OF NICELY CRAFTED ENTERTAINMENT, DESCRIBES THE THINKING BEHIND NCE'S SEMINAL STRATEGY GAME, **TIME OF DEFIANCE**:*

'Artificial Life concerns itself with capturing lifelike behaviour by creating large populations of simple systems out of whose interactions more complex behaviour will emerge that none of the individual systems are aware of. Because it is "lifelike" behaviour that we are after, we call it Artificial Life.

'Artificial Life is a thoroughly bottom-up, inside-out development philosophy that draws heavily on the phrase "if you build it, they will come". The joy of this approach is that you don't need to understand the problem in order to solve it. You just need to model the appropriate low-level building blocks out of which desired behaviour can emerge. The cost is control. The gains are substantial: you end up with scalable, reliable, self-consistent, plausible, and vastly complex gaming environments that adapt themselves over time to meet the needs of the players inside them.'

We spoke to the people at Nicely Crafted about what they look for in strategy game design and their goals in creating the next generation of strategy gaming.

***MARK ASHTON**, Senior Producer:* 'I'm one of those people who think there is still a place for good turn-based strategy games. I'm sure there are many who disagree with me. Admittedly a rea-ltime game against other human players is hard to beat, especially when the action is getting frenetic and there is more room for error.'

***ED BLINCOE**, Director of Sales and Marketing:* 'An RTS needs all the elements of economy and exploration as well as warfare to create an air of realism. How those elements are implemented and how deep in the heart of the game they should be depends on the type of game you're intending to create. Will it be heavy on the battle and tactical front or more of an exploration and mini-attack angle?'

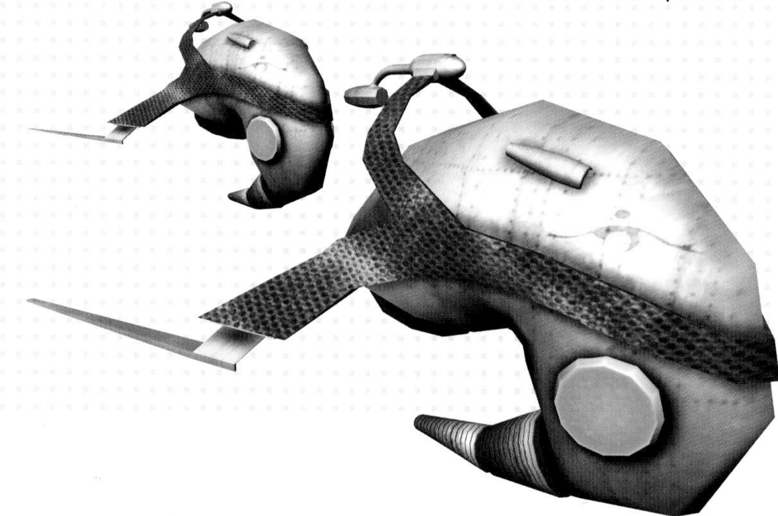

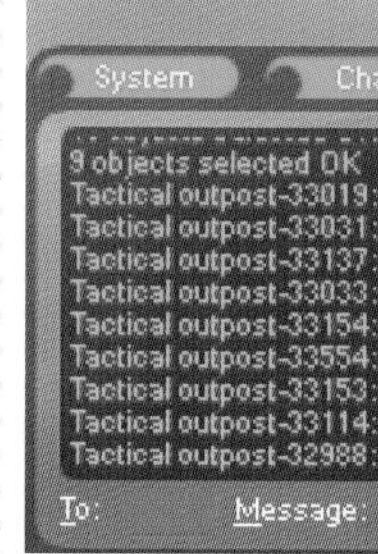

*All pictures from **Time of Defiance**.*

Scores
Summary
Session
Players
Empire view
N
Fryeya
Range 7.21km
Free floating camera
Dobbsekkian
Range 1.68km
Chat status
Visible to all
Help
F1
Disconnect

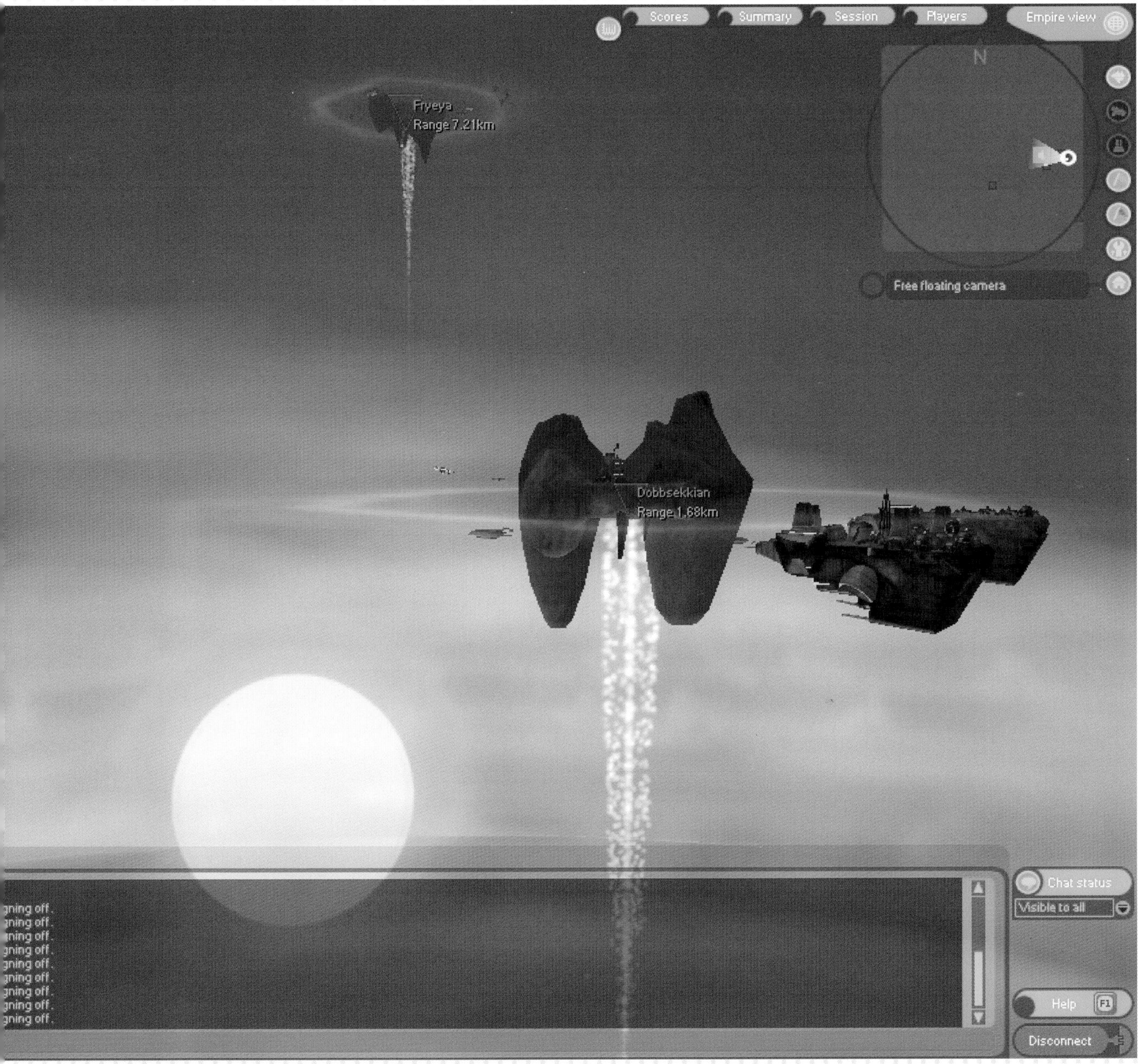

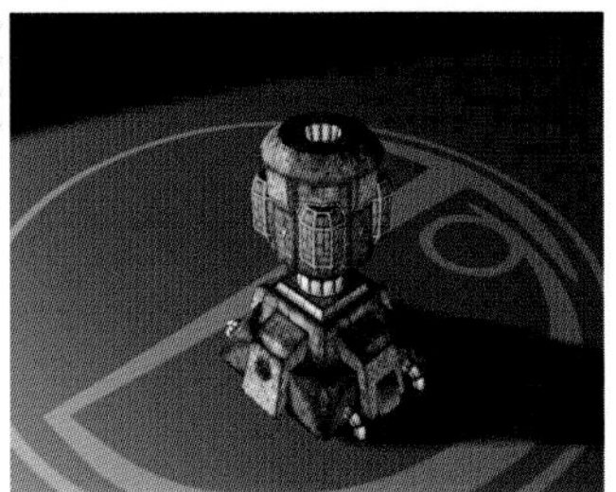

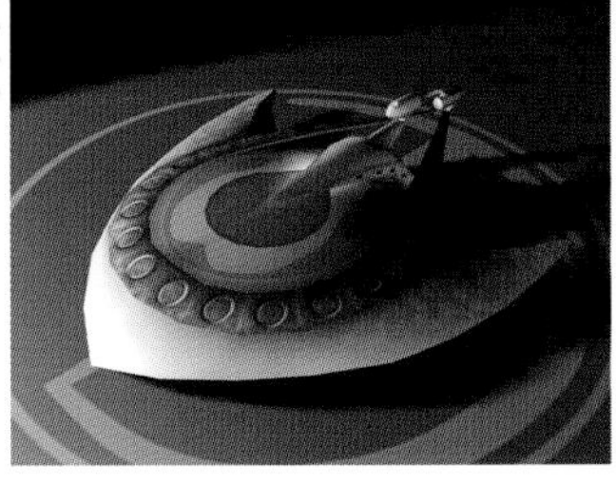

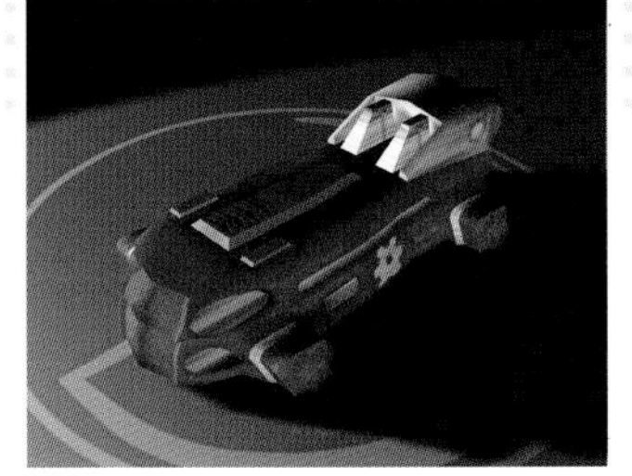

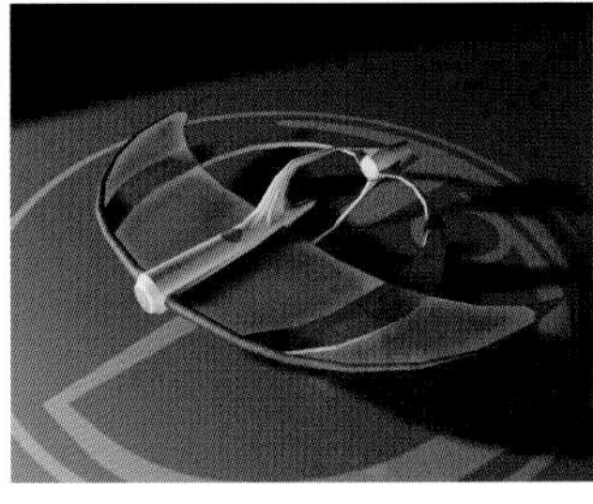

A WORLD OF DIFFERENCE 2

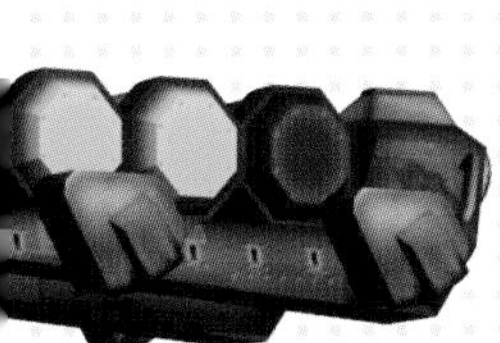

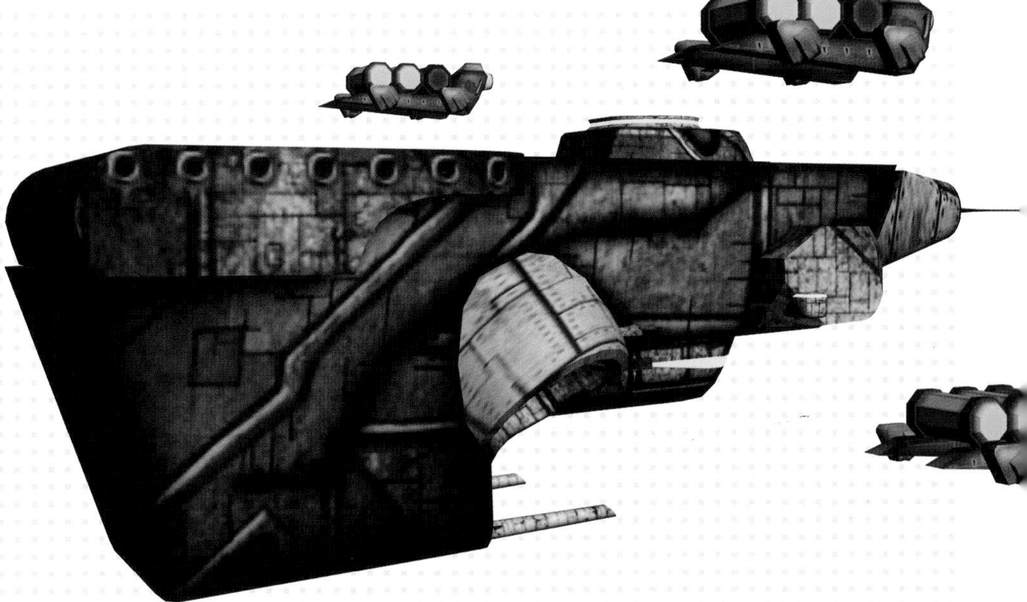

'The scale of the **Time of Defiance** playing arena is very large,' points out **Ed Blincoe**. 'Our games are played out over a 4000 x 4000 kilometer (2500 x 2500 mile) area. Simply travelling from one side of the map to the other would take days, and the players would need to plan ahead or they'll run out of fuel long before they made it across. We have implemented other ways to cross the map, such as a Quantum Foam Gate, which can transport a player instantaneously to any point of the map, at a cost. This means that logistics, which on the whole has been ignored in earlier strategy wargames, is now becoming a significant factor.'

MARK ASHTON: 'You could have an RTS where the whole map is known in advance, and I also think it would be very possible to have an RTS where you controlled just a single unit. The base-building elements, too, are not necessary, and there are some fine strategy games out there that don't entail building up an economy. But when all of these elements are mixed in together, I think it allows a number of ways for the players to make their mark. Penetrating the fog of war, or building up a stockpile of resources, or laying down a strong settlement, can all swing the war – as long as you pick the right strategy compared to your opponents.'

FIVE HUNDRED FOES

ED BLINCOE: 'Online is the way forward for the RTS genre. Artificial intelligence is a long way from being able to counter players' moves in an intuitive manner. The only way to get around this is for players to play against each other. *Time of Defiance* allows upwards of 500 players to test themselves against each other.'

MARK ASHTON: 'Player-on-player has always been the best way to enjoy a strategy game. The game can have a lifetime of years if played among a peer group of similar ability, as new tactics are learned and countertactics developed. A single-player RTS is more about finding ways to exploit the AI by working around it, which although fun is a different kind of game altogether.'

AT WAR WITH NATURE

MARK ASHTON: 'Most RTS games, whether 2D or 3D, have had the concepts of impassable and selectively passable terrain, or terrain that slows certain types of movement. With the advent of 3D RTS we tend to see things like terrain advantage becoming more important. It would be great to see true fully deformable landscapes that cratered and changed as the game progresses, but the hardware is still a little way from being able to create that sort of system. It will be great, though, and I think new uses for terrain and other environmental effects will emerge from it.'

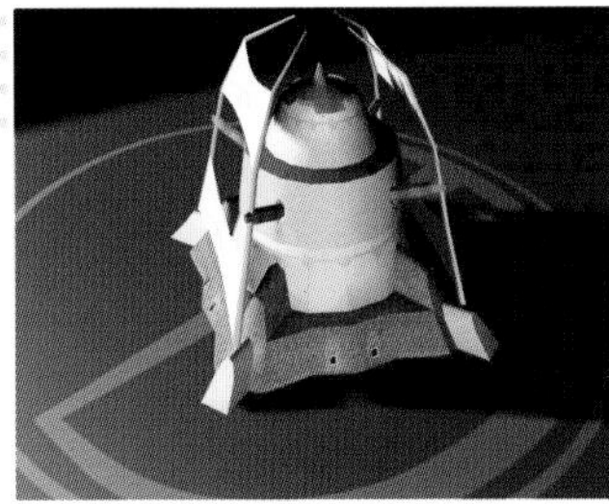

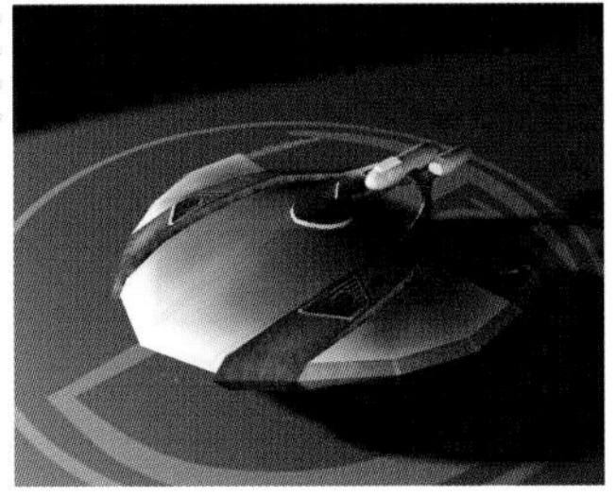

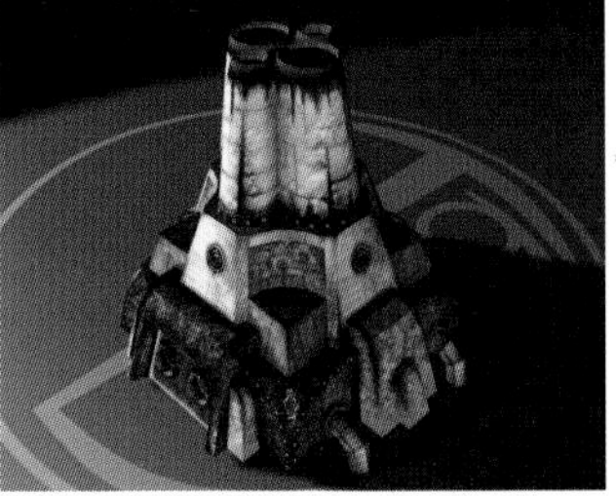

ED BLINCOE: 'This is something we've been looking at for some time now. *Time of Defiance* takes place on islands floating in space. This gives scope for all kind of environmental effects such as magnetic storms, lightning, meteor strikes and wormholes. The last two are already implemented, with the rest following as the year rolls on. These won't just be pretty special effects but will have a direct impact on how a battle is played out.'

IT'S THE ECONOMY

MARK ASHTON: 'An economic strategy is important in a number of RTS games, and it opens up the whole area of grand strategy – namely whether you win the war by outfighting your foe or by outproducing him.'

ED BLINCOE: 'The player needs to earn their way forward. Whether it be constructing warships, miners or buildings, players need to know that they have to be shrewd and manage their empire effectively.'

MARK ASHTON: 'You should design in as many resources as your players can handle. When we get to talking about games with truly strategic-scale maps, that doesn't have to mean very many resources, however. In *Time of Defiance* we use two main construction resources for ships (wood and metal) and just with those two coming in from different locations, and in different amounts, it means a player has to plan the best way to use and move their resources. An island with a surplus of 1000 units of wood sitting in silos is no good if your home island is in desperate need of that wood. Typically, flying those resources in a large transporter can take many hours, so planning does pay off. That and keeping an eye on future resource requirements around your empire.'

ED BLINCOE: 'Logistics is a critical consideration in real-world military planning. There are always resources, and they always have to be moved around somehow. In game terms it's best to offer the player several different options for handling supply, which all have strengths and weaknesses. Players tend to try them all out and then go for the option that suits them.'

MARK ASHTON: 'Scale matters for other reasons too. If you buy a game expecting to command Alexander's vast armies, and once it's fired up you find you've got a control of few dozen men on a football field then I think you'd be rightly disappointed.'

A WORLD OF DIFFERENCE 3

*'We developed a complete timeline and history of our world of Nespanona,' explains **Ed Blincoe**. 'We then looked at the timeline and found a suitable period for the game to happen within. This means the game has a history and we at Nicely Crafted Entertainment know what happens next and where the game is heading. All of the battles, empires and happenings within **Time of Defiance** will constantly push this story forward.'*

A WORLD OF DIFFERENCE

'Most RTS games don't actually model ammunition for each unit,' says Mark Ashton. 'Sometimes a nicer game can be made by stepping away from reality, sometimes by stepping towards reality.'

PURISM OR PROFUSION?

MARK ASHTON: 'The question of whether to go for a massive range of possible units or just a few finely balanced ones is tricky. The purist in me would opt for the latter, but on the other hand it can be nice to feel you have a breadth of choices to make when constructing your units -- and ultimately your strategy. For experienced players I think new units are nearly always welcome since they add new possibilities, but for someone just starting out on a game it could be a bit overwhelming having too large a choice, and no context or knowledge to know which is best to use for what purpose.'

ED BLINCOE: 'And after all, who says you can't have it both ways? Our players choose for themselves how deep into the game they want to go. Initially a player can build around 15 vehicle units along with around the same again number of static units – mines, silos, and so on. However, with a little cash they can buy loads more, and with a lot of cash they can buy a coloniser from another race and start building their units, too.'

THE POWER OF DIPLOMACY

MARK ASHTON: 'Alliance is an interesting factor in real politics and warfare. Yet traditionally it hasn't featured much in strategy games because of the brief game duration,

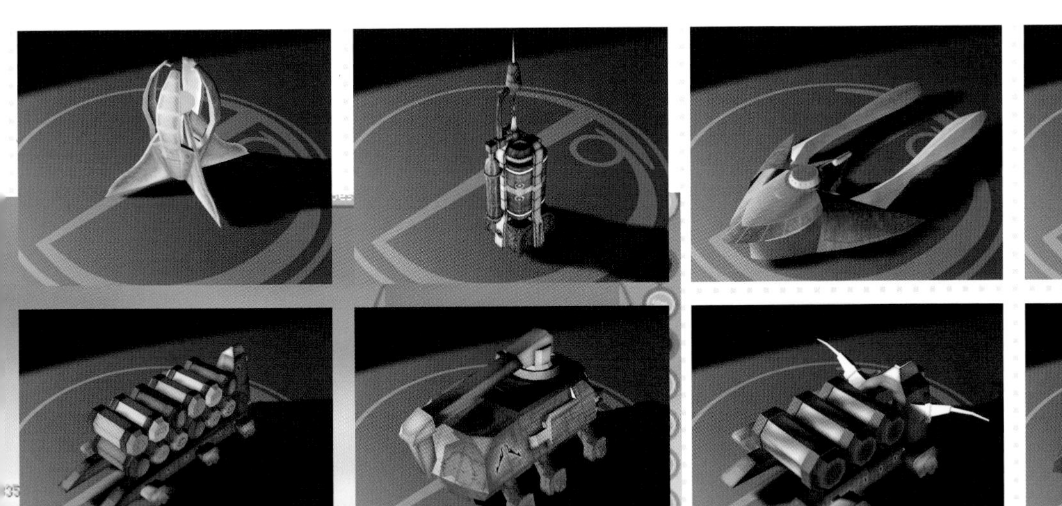

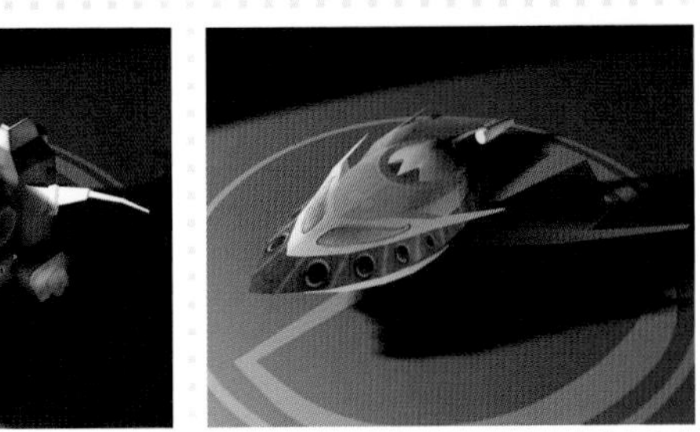

limited benefits from trade, the fact that the games are zero-sum, and so on. *Time of Defiance* doesn't have those problems. With games lasting weeks rather than minutes, there is plenty of time for the payback on helping an ally or reaping revenge. There are no witless computer opponents clogging up the place – everyone you meet is human, and unpredictable, because of it. A strong allied group can achieve more than a strong individual but can also attract the jealousy of those who aren't reaping its benefit. In *Time of Defiance* I have seen alliances rise just to counter a potential world-spanning alliance, and temporary alliances formed to defend against a hostile neighbour. The human element is something that's been missing in most strategy games until now.'

ED BLINCOE: 'In a game that lasts for weeks and supports hundreds of players, you can't afford to ignore the others around you. Strong empires have been pecked apart by a horde of individually weaker empires because they didn't talk to them, and weak empires sow seeds of mistrust against strong empires with a word or two in the right places. Treachery, honour, and propaganda, as well as traditional exploration, management and combat, are all vital parts of *Time of Defiance*.'

GLOSSARY

AI (Artificial Intelligence): The simulation of human intelligence by a computer. In games, AI refers more specifically to the behaviour of computer-controlled opponents or allies, and how this affects gameplay.

Artillery: A military unit that uses large-calibre weaponry. In a strategy game, this usually means a unit with high attack characteristics, but often low speed and/or defence capabilities. Typical artillery units would include catapults, cannons or missile launchers, depending on the setting.

Balance: In games design, a design goal, where the designer attempts to achieve a balance between the game being too easy or too difficult. In strategy games, the designer also needs to balance individual units so that they're neither too weak nor too powerful against other units.

Base: An encampment or fortification belonging to the player or his opponent. In most strategy games, bases provide manufacturing facilities. In many cases, losing all the bases will result in failing the mission or losing the game.

Campaign: A collection of missions, linked by a narrative, historical period, or theme.

Cavalry: A military unit consisting of troops on horseback or armoured vehicles. These units would usually have high attack characteristics and a high movement speed. Typical cavalry units would include knights, armoured cars and tanks, depending on the setting.

Combined arms: In a battle or military campaign, the combination and coordination of different troop types in order to achieve set objectives.

Fog of war: Originally, a term that alludes to the confusion and uncertainty characterizing mass combat. In games, it has come to refer to a means of hiding enemy actions from the player unless a player-controlled unit is within visual range of their troops.

FPS (First-Person Shooter): A popular genre of action game, in which the player battles through a hostile environment using a mass of destructive weaponry. The game is played from the direct point-of-view of the protagonist.

Gameplay: A loose term describing the mechanics of a game and the experience of the player as he plays it.

Harvesting: In strategy games, the process of resource gathering by automated units. This might be mining, tree felling or spice harvesting, according to the setting, but the effect is the gathering of currency or resources in order to produce new units or buildings.

Infantry: Foot soldiers. Infantry are the basic unit of most strategy games, being cheap to produce and effective when used in large groups and tight formations. Typical infantry units would include phalanx, footmen, pikemen or space-marines, depending on period and setting.

Interface: The layer of screen icons, menus, and mouse and keyboard controls that allows the player to interact with the game.

Level: A single mission, map or section of a game.

Management game: A popular style of game, in which the player builds and manages facilities and employees in order to achieve mission goals. The player might manage a city, a zoo, a theme park or a space colony, but the overall presentation and game mechanics work in roughly the same way.

Massive multiplayer: An online game in which dozens or even hundreds of players can participate simultaneously.

Mission: A single objective or a series of objectives detailed at the start of the level. In some game types (strategy games, military simulations) missions are virtually synonymous with levels.

Morale: The simulation of 'fear' or 'courage' in a strategy game. Units with high morale are more likely to stand firm against a charge or rush into the fray for maximum effect. Units with low morale may rout when attacked or refuse to join battle.

Multiplayer: A game in which more than one player participates at a time. Multiplayer games may be cooperative (the players work together to achieve a single goal) or competitive (the players battle for supremacy). The most successful strategy games have large multiplayer followings.

Neural net: A technology that simulates the workings of the human brain to allow a computer to recognize patterns and learn simple or complex tasks.

Pathfinding: The ability of units or characters, while under computer control, to find their way from one position to another. Good pathfinding means that the unit or character should take the shortest and safest route. Poor pathfinding was a constant problem with early role-playing and strategy games, as characters struggled to get through doors or took the long route across the caustic swamp rather than the shortcut across the grassy meadows.

Physics system: A system of in-game sub-programs designed to simulate real-world physics within the game world. Objects move, tumble and fall according to the effects of momentum, weight, friction and gravity, adding to the realism and opening up new game mechanics.

Realtime: In general computing terms, a process or display that updates from moment to moment as the user interacts with it. In gaming terms, realtime means that the action takes place in real time as the player interacts with the game world, rather than pausing for periods so that the player can take decisions, or taking a turn-based form.

Resource: A material or energy that needs to be gathered by the player or an opponent in order to build facilities or units.

RPG (Role-Playing Game): A game genre, adapted from the classic tabletop 'Dungeons & Dragons' style of game, in which the player takes on a character and goes adventuring through a particular game world. Typically, the player tackles quests or explores levels, battling creatures or solving mysteries. By doing so, he or she wins experience points to increase the character's capabilities, and discovers weapons or objects that can make them more powerful.

RTS (Realtime Strategy): A sub-genre of strategy, which has risen to become the dominant form of the genre. The player builds and controls their forces in realtime, increasing the pace of the action but forcing the player to think and act quickly in order to succeed.

Scripting: A means of controlling events or the behaviour of computer-controlled characters by defining branching chains of cause and effect that result from the actions of the player.

Super unit: A powerful unit in a strategy game, capable of wiping out lesser units with ease.

Tech tree: A structure that controls progress from one technology to a better technology, enabling the player to create better facilities or more powerful units. For example, developing iron-working and horseback riding, then creating a stables facility, might enable the player to create a knight.

Terrain: The landscape of a strategy game. In early strategy games, terrain had little effect apart from slowing down troops as they tried to cross it. In modern strategy games, the height and type of the ground will have an impact on everything from the speed of movement to the effectiveness of missile weapons.

Trigger-point: In gaming terms, a position on the level map which causes an event when the player wanders into it. This might be an attack by hostile forces, a pre-scripted story sequence, or a sudden change in the conditions or landscape.

Turn-based: A game that follows traditional tabletop boardgames, wargames or RPGs. Players or opponents take it in turns to move, fight or otherwise act, with the action pausing while any decisions are made.

Upgrade: An advance that, when applied to a unit, makes it more powerful and effective at its job, or able to take on new tasks. For example, in a historical wargame, basic footmen could be upgraded to pikemen, making them more dangerous in battle and more effective in a defensive position.

Wonder: A term that has become the generic description for a building or event that confers bonuses on the player or provides an objective in a mission. Stems from the 'Wonders of the World' in the original *Civilization,* where the player could build the likes of 'The Great Library' or 'The Manhattan Project' and so gain benefits for his or her civilization.

INDEX

A
1503 AD: The New World 39, 50–1, 63, 82,123
2020 Knife Edge 32, 46, 48
3D, freedom of 32–3,
3D environment 31
3D physicality 111
Africa Korps vs Desert Rats 112
Against Rome 11, 98
Age of Empires 20, 45, 61, 65, 100, 102–3, 104, 126
Age of Kings 82, 104
Age of Mythology 32, 52, 54, 55, 58, 61, 65, 66, 71, 72, 102, 104
Akella 97, 109, 116
Alien Nations 73
alliance 138–9
Alpha Centauri 17, 39
Ancient Art of War, The 35, 81
animation 118
Art of Magic 90
artificial intelligence 33, 35, 103, 104, 135
artificial life 29, 132
  based strategy 28
artificial opponents 34–41
Ashton, Mark 19, 99, 132, 135, 136
attractor points 27, 28
  strategic roles 28
attributes 13, 14, 17, 97
  balanced 23
  combination of 27
autonomous heroes 94

B
balance 14, 17, 23, 96–7, 104
balanced units 104
base, the 64–5
  single 71
battalion tabs 109
battle, site of 100
BC 123
Belanger, Danny 35, 89, 101, 131
Bewsher, Charlie 70
Black & White 57, 90, 124
Black & White 2 46
Black Cactus Games 35, 70, 75, 83, 88
Blinco, Ed 135, 136, 137
Blitzkrieg: Burning Horizon 59
Blizzard 16, 26, 32, 59, 70, 91, 111
Bright, Walter et al. 68
bullet time 46
Bullfrog 58, 63, 89, 90

C
campaigns 98–101
Cavedog 114
CDV Software 11, 78, 83, 118–19
chain of command 95, 109
changing conditions 43
Chicago 1930 34, 35, 99
choices 115
Civilization 59, 63, 74
Civilization 3 76, 77, 83
Climax 7, 13, 90, 99, 107
Codename 11, 13, 78, 83, 118–19
Codo International 23, 40, 47, 71
combined arms 22–5
Command & Conquer: Generals 7, 17, 19, 73, 81, 90
Commandos 69
Commandos 3 79, 123
complex design 17
Condorcet Cycle 25
conflict 9, 53
consoles, future of 126
control interface 90
Cossacks 117
Creative Assembly 27
Crusader Kings 63, 79, 89, 111
cyclical path 41
cyclical relationships 23

D
Day 1 Studios 21
Deactivation 116
Deep Red 120
defence 48–49
design 86–139
  killers 17
Desperados 2 44, 101, 122
dialectical heroes 95
Digital Reality, 7, 27, 42, 43, 73, 84, 107, 112
Disciples II: The Dark Prophecy 37, 99, 112–13, 121
dominant strategies 17, 23, 97
dominated strategies 17, 24
Dune 2 89
Dungeon Keeper 55, 58, 89
Dungeon Keeper 2 62, 90
dynamic balance 97
Dynasty Warriors 115

E
Earth & Beyond 64, 107
economy 135, 136
Eidos 32, 46, 85
Electronic Arts 17, 64, 73, 81
Elixir Studios 32, 43, 95, 108–9, 110
Empire Earth 28, 74
Empire: Wargame of the Century 68
Ensemble Studios 18, 32, 52, 54, 65, 71, 72, 102–3, 104
environmental
  conditions 45
environmental effects 129, 135, 136
environmental factors 31, 113, 128
Evil Genius 43, 110
exhaustible resources 58

F
fantasy setting 122
fear 119
Firaxis 7, 17, 39, 59, 63, 73, 113
Firefly 33, 40, 41, 45, 60, 66, 67, 115, 117
first-order strategies 14
flowcharted checklists 36
flying units 31, 32
fog of war 68–71, 91, 135
Fuller, Buckminster 91
future, the 130–1

G
game balance 96
game identity 111
gameplay 114–15
  realism of 113
  style of 112
Gangland 125, 126, 128
GCS Game World 117
Gettysburg 7, 107, 11
global stocks 55
graphics 112, 113,
Gregerson, Adam 125–9

H
Haegemonia 7, 42, 43, 73, 84, 107
harvested resources 55
harvester units 55
harvesters 89
harvesting 55, 56
heroes 92
hierarchical games 107
  autonomous 94
  dialectical 95
higher-order strategies 14
Hill, Avalon 64, 77
historical games 112
Homeworld 2 33, 101, 106, 107

I
Impossible Creatures 20, 28, 31, 115
Incunabula 77
Independent Arts 11, 98
inexhaustible resources 58
infection 82
intercommunicating nodes 37
interface 88–91
  and heroes 95
  intrusive 109
IS Games 10, 38, 91
Intrepid 123
invasion 82

J
Jowood 73, 86–7, 93

K
KD Lab 30, 80

L
Lanchester's Second Law *see* N-squared Law
landscape 100
Laser Squad: Nemesis 23, 40, 47, 71
layers 37, 39, 74
level design 98
levels 98–101
Lindgren, Fredrik 19, 23, 57, 85
Lionhead 46, 57, 124
localized resources 57

M
Magic & Mayhem 13
Massive Assault 15, 22, 111
Mathematica 13
MechAssault 21
MediaMobsters 125, 126
medieval warfare 117
Meier, Sid 39, 107, 114
Mindscape 76
Moore's Law 108
morale effects 119
movies 108
  Alexander 131
  Band of Brothers 131
  Lord of the Rings 108
  Saving Private Ryan 109
  Troy 131
multiplayer games 107
multiple levels 89
multiple resources 58
Murray, David and Barry 35

N
N-dimensional space 27
N-squared Law 45
neural nets 37, 39
New World Computing 74
Nicely Crafted Entertainment 19, 99, 132
Nival Interactive 19, 23, 27, 59, 64, 71, 109, 131

O
'officer interface' 95
open game environment 100
othogonal attribute design 104

P
Paradox Entertainment 19, 23, 57, 63, 79, 85, 89, 111
pathfinding 35
peace 50–85
Pérez, Ignacio 82
Perimeter 30, 80
personality (of opponent) 35
Phenomic 7, 109
Platoon 27
playing experience 126
population limit effect 61
Populous 3 90
positive feedback device 97
Prince of Persia 115
Privateer's Bounty 97, 109
Project Nomads 21
'pudding of monsters' effect 89
Pyro Studios 54, 69, 79, 82, 123

R
'Races' 97
Rapscallions 123
Raydon Labs 21
realism 113
realtime 45, 46–7, 82, 85, 108, 125
realtime game 43, 46, 49, 53
Red Alert 126, 128
Relic 20, 28, 31, 33, 101, 115, 106, 107
renewable resources 58
Republic: the Revolution 32, 95, 108–9
resource cost 14
resources 53–61
  exhaustible/
  as forts 70
  harvested 55
  inexhaustible 58
  localized 57
  multiple 58
  renewable 58
  self-generating 56
  stockpile of 134
  storage of 61
  and territory 62
  and upgrades 73
Robin Hood 49
Rourke's Drift 108

S
S2 Games 13, 67, 130
Savage 15, 67, 130
scale 106–9, 136
script-based systems 40
  drawbacks of 40
scripted solutions 36
scripted system 39
self-generating resources 56
settings 120–3
  fantasy 32, 122
  historical 121
  sci-fi 122
shadow resources 59
Shogun Total War 27, 100
Silent Storm 19, 23, 27, 65, 7, 109, 131
Simpson, Toby 132
Sims, The 131
slow motion 46
sound 118
Space Colony 41, 66, 115
Spaceword Ho 74
spawning units 61, 62, 69, 103, 104
Spellbound 34, 35, 44, 49, 99, 101, 122
Spellforce 7, 86–7, 93,108
spies 70–1
static balance 97
Stonkers 97
storage of resources 61
strategy 6–7
Strategy First 37, 99, 112–13, 121
Stronghold 33, 40, 45, 60, 66, 67, 117
style 110–13,
Sunflowers 39, 50–1, 63, 82, 123
super units 18–21
supply 80–5, 136
supply lines 80, 82, 85

T
tactics 10, 20, 23, 24, 53
Tartan Army 107
tech tree 73, 75, 77
technology 24, 72–5, 91, 107
  retro-grav 79
tension 11, 95
terrain 23, 25, 31, 33, 43, 69, 128, 135
terror tactics 118–19
Thermopylae 108
time 107
Time of Defiance 11, 132–3, 134–5, 136–7, 138–9
Total Annihilation 56, 114
trade 77
trade-off 55, 58, 85, 126
trigger point 40
turn-based (time) 82, 132
Twynholm, Paul 7, 91, 99, 107

U
upgrades 15, 61, 72, 73, 74, 75, 76, 77, 100

V
variable time-rates 107
Vegas! Make it Big 120
virtual units 40
visual style 111, 113

W
war 8–49
  medieval 117
  and morale effects
  psychological dimensions of 118
  realtime terror tactics of 118
Warcraft 19, 20, 59, 65, 66, 81, 90, 91
Warcraft 2 70, 97, 111
Warcraft 3 16, 26, 32,59, 97
Wargaming.net 15, 22, 111
War Times 10, 38, 91
War Wind 76
Warrior Kings Battles 35, 75, 83, 85, 88
Warzone 2100, 85
weather effects 25, 30, 129
Westwood 89
Wolfram, Stephen 13
World War II 59, 121

X
XCOM: Enemy Unknown 75

Z
zoom level 107

ACKNOWLEDGEMENTS

WE'D LIKE TO THANK ALL WHO HAVE HELPED IN THE MAKING OF THIS BOOK WITH ADVICE, IMAGES, QUOTATIONS AND MORAL SUPPORT. IN PARTICULAR, AND IN NO SPECIAL ORDER, THANKS TO:

Mark Ashton, Ed Blincoe, and Toby and Ben Simpson of Nicely Crafted Entertainment.
Danny Belanger, Mark Cecere and Kelly Ekins of Strategy First.
Stephanie Malham at Digital Jesters.
Kelley Gilmore at Fireaxis.
Alexander Shcherbakov at Akella.
Evelyn Reina at CDV.
Gabor Feher and Tamás Daubner at Digital Reality.
Paul Twynholm and Dawn Beasley at Climax.
Nick Katselapov at Wargaming.net.
Andreas Speer at Spellbound.
Rafael Alcala at Legend Studios.
Poppy Reeve-Tucker at Elixir Studios.
John Johnson at Relic.
Fredrik Lindgren at Paradox.
Lisa Pearce and George Wang at Blizzard Entertainment.
Kathryne Wahl at Interplay.
Ignacio Pérez and Íñigo Vinós at Pyro Studios.
Adam R. L. Gregersen and Jacob Nordahl at MediaMobsters.
Lance Hoke at Ensemble Studios.
Charlie Bewsher, Black Cactus Games.
Marina Guseva at K D Lab.
Julian Gollop at Codo Technologies Ltd.
Darren Thompson at Firefly Studios Ltd.
Ernest W. Adams.
Dmitry Kolpakov at Nival Interactive.
Lynn Vanbesien at Larian Studios
Andrew Rollings.
www.mobygames.com
www.military-quotes.com

We'll end on a very insightful piece of advice that applies to game designers working in all genres:

'IMMERSION – A LOT OF GAME CREATORS NEGLECT THIS CRUCIAL ASPECT. WHO IS THE PLAYER? WHAT IS THE SETTING? WHAT IS THE PLAYER MOTIVATION? GAMES CAN NO LONGER RELY ON A SIMPLE PRETEXT FOR STORY; DESIGNERS AND GAME WRITERS MUST WORK HARD TO CREATE INTERESTING AND INVOLVING SETTINGS. WHY SHOULD THE PLAYER BUY YOUR GAME? WHAT DID YOU DO TO CREATE A UNIQUE EXPERIENCE? MOVIES AND GAMES ARE CONVERGING TOWARDS THE SAME POINT. STRONG SETTINGS AND CHARACTERS MUST BE CONCEIVED THAT WILL AWAKEN THE PLAYER'S SENSE OF WONDER, HIS INNER CHILD. THE PLAYER MUST UNDERSTAND WHO HE IS IN THE GAME, WHAT HE IS DOING, AND MOST IMPORTANTLY CARE ABOUT HIS ACTIONS.' DANNY BELANGER, STRATEGY FIRST